PROTECTING YOUR LOVED ONES
Security Awareness for Parents and Adults

Orlando Wilson

Beware of having too many friends, for surely only someone who knows you can harm you.

- IMAM ALI (AS)

Cover designed by Orlando Wilson

Orlando Wilson
Visit my website at www.tohff.com

Printed in the United States of America

Proof reading services by Dahlia Allen – English Language Services

First Printing: July 2018
Orlando Wilson

ISBN- 9781717755933

CONTENTS

INTRODUCTION

This book has been written to give parents and adults guidance on how to enhance the security and safety of their loved ones. The information in this handbook is simple, common sense, easy to apply and has been proven to be effective.

These days the threats to a person's personal security and safety are extremely varied and for a parent looking after small children or teenagers the threats they need to be aware of are constantly developing. This handbook will help you be aware of and be able to identify potential security and safety threats. By being aware of potential threats you can then educate your family on how to avoid them and have plans in place in case you need to deal with any issues.

At the time of writing this handbook I have personally been involved in the international security industry for over 29 years and the main thing I have heard from the victims of crime is that they never thought it would happen to them. Likewise, I have had people attend my classes who dismiss advice because "It will never happen to them". Well, I will let you in on a big secret... Crime can affect anyone and everyone!

These days such things as substance abuse, domestic violence, rape, stalkers and terrorism can affect people from all backgrounds, all social classes and in all locations. The topics covered in this handbook apply to parents and children alike and I have tried to emphasize some of the points with stories from real people and situations. The scope of this handbook is wide and touches on social issues that even if they don't apply to you directly, they can affect you indirectly, due to the circumstances of family members or close friends.

You will see that I am very much a fan of planning in order to avoid problems, dealing with problems is something we want to avoid. Now, these plans do not have to be full blown military briefings. A simple, relaxed family discussion on potential issues and what to do if the issue occurs should suffice. If someone does not want to listen because "It will never happen to them", then find some related stories or videos online of actual incidents to help emphasize your point.

With everything in life education is the key, as you read through this book highlight what applies to your situation and develop your plans, procedures and precautions as needed. There is no magic fix for good personal or family security, it's something you need to think about, analyze, put procedures in place and constantly review.

My aim with this handbook is to get you thinking and highlight potential threats that you may have overlooked as well as give you some practical advice on how to help minimalize them.

Stay safe,

Orlando Wilson
Cyprus - 2018

SECURITY AWARENESS

Everyone should understand the basics of personal security awareness. Ultimately your personal security, the security of your family and your assets is your responsibility. In most cases you call the police to report a crime, which means the crime has already taken place; your aim is to prevent the crime from happening. Also, you want to ensure that if someone calls the police it is not because of your actions or those of a family member; it is very easy these days, especially for children and teens to get themselves into serious trouble that can ruin the rest of their lives.

It is a sad fact that in many countries crime is part of everyday life. I believe that everyone should be aware of the threats and know how to identify and avoid potentially hostile situations. In this chapter I want to give you some basic tips on how you can be more security aware and able to protect yourselves and your families.

Let me start by posing a question... When do you think people first started to be security aware...? I would say since people first inhabited the earth... Since the beginning of history all kings and rulers have had their bodyguards and the main difference between their tactics now and two thousand years ago is that these days they have guns and cars, while back then they had swords and horses. So, nothing we are going to discuss is new nor are the techniques complicated, it is basic awareness and common sense.

Minding your own business

A lot of problems I see people encountering usually start with them getting involved in other people's personal issues and dramas. Whether they are doing this to try to help, be a Good Samaritan or just to be nosy it is irrelevant.

For me the main principal of personal security is to avoid problems and hostile situations by understanding the threats and planning to avoid them. If you are a parent, any problems you have because of your actions are also going to affect your children. Most of us have enough problems to deal with on a daily basis so why put more on your plate by getting involved in others' drama. If you are going help someone ensure that any negative repercussions are not going to affect you or your family.

I am sure many reading this will find my attitude harsh, well it is, very much so, but why? Well, maybe I have dealt with too many problems, my own, my friends' and clients'. And to be honest with you, after going out of your way to help most people they will not be grateful, these days most will see it as an entitlement and will try to take advantage. The favor you did once will become expected the next time they have a problem, and when you refuse they will try to make you out as the wrong doer.

We have to be very selective of who we call friends and let into our lives; until someone is well known and proven trustworthy, don't trust them. I am sure you the reader know of or have heard of situations where family members have conned, betrayed or caused major issues for each other, so if you can't trust family then you'd be stupid to put 100% faith in strangers.

Relationships develop over time, what people say means little these days, actions and behavior prove the real person. Assess your friends and family, forget blind loyalty, and categorize them for their trustworthiness, reliability and potential for causing you problems. If you understand how much you can trust someone and what to expect from their behavior, then you should never put yourself in a situation with them beyond this limit. If you know what to expect from someone's behavior, then they should never disappoint you, because you should never trust them past their limitations.

This is a story told to me by a client during one of my classes; due to him and his family doing the right thing their action could have caused them major problems. This client and his family were very nice people, he and his wife had very good professions, which means they had a lot to lose.

While on a family vacation and driving through a rural part of the US they saw a girl in her early 20's standing on the side of the road trying to get a ride to the nearest town. So, being nice people, they pulled over... The girl was distressed and explained she had had an argument with her boyfriend who had thrown her out of the car and left. The client and his wife felt sorry for the girl and gave her a lift to the next town, bought her lunch and ensured she was Ok before they left her, they are good people...

Good people but very naïve since this girl could have caused them big problems... 1. She was distressed and admitted she had had a hostile argument with a boyfriend... What was the reason for the argument? Domestic situations are very unpredictable, what if the boyfriend had come back looking for her, what if he was aggravated and armed, the client had just put his family in the firing line... 2. Was she under the influence of drugs, did she have drugs on her, who knows, and they let her into their car with them and their children. If they were pulled over by the police for whatever reason and the girl did have drugs on her, what would she have done with them... Dropped them in the car? If the cop saw or smelled drugs in the car, searched it and found them, where would everybody most likely be going? Well, the adults to jail and the children to Child Services... Hopefully the client could get someone to hire a bondsman to bail them out of jail, then he could get an attorney to deal with the case and get his children back... Hopefully he would beat the drug charge and the arrest would not affect his and his wife's professional licenses and future employment prospects... 3. How did they know the girl did not have warrants, was wanted by the police or was an armed criminal? They didn't, they were just very lucky.

I am sure some of you reading this will think I am taking things to the extreme however everything I mentioned is very viable. So, what would I have done, most probably kept driving, no way as a single man would I have picked up an unaccompanied female. Why, because all she has to do is make an accusation of sexual assault and I would have major problems. I will talk more about this type of issue later...

So, what could the client and family have done to help the girl and stay safe at the same time? They should have called the police and reported they had found the girl and were taking her to a town, KYA... The dispatcher would have advised the client if there were known issue and to wait for an officer... The girl could have been wanted or reported missing. If the girl did not want the police called, that would have been a big red flag... They should at least have asked her and visually checked that she had no drugs or weapons before letting her in the car. If she objected, we have another red flag...

Hopefully you can see from that simple example how you need to look at things and don't believe what you're told, analyze situations. By all means help people but do not place you and your loved ones at risk!

Counter surveillance

Now, counter surveillance may sound like something that only the James Bond's of the world should know about, but it is in fact a very simple skill to master. The reason you need to understand counter-surveillance is to identify anyone who has you under surveillance. In nearly all burglaries, muggings, robberies or kidnappings the criminals will put their target under surveillance to assess their target's routines and the level of personal security.

Professional surveillance operatives put their targets into three categories: unaware, aware and professional. Most people, I would say at least 75%, fall into the unaware category, you can follow them around all day and they won't realize you're there. Try it the next time you're out at the mall. About 24% of people would fall into the aware category and would realize, after a while if someone was watching or following them. The 1% left would fall into the professional category; they take active counter surveillance measures and would spot people acting suspicious, watching, or following them. So, I expect most people reading this article are in the unaware category but by the time you finish reading this book there is no reason not to be in the professional category.

I am going to highlight some general considerations for personal security counter-surveillance and detail some simple but effective street drills that will enable you to identify if you are under surveillance. You can start training while you're reading this chapter; look around where you are now, if you're in an office look out the window. Are there any people hanging around on the street or sitting in parked cars for no apparent reason? If they are still there in 30 minutes and there is no logical reason, what are they up to, what's their body language saying, are they being over observant? People don't hang around the streets and sit in parked cars for no reason, unless they are on surveillance or up to something!

Learning to read people's body language is an extremely important skill, if someone is on surveillance or looking to commit a crime, chances are they will be acting differently than those around them. Most people do not pay attention to their surroundings, so if someone is over observant what are they up to? When you are out at the mall or in a restaurant, watch the people around you and try to identify what mood they are in or what type of discussion they are having with others. It should be easy to identify if a man and a woman are on a romantic date or two business people are having a heated discussion. When in a coffee shop try to determine what people are looking at on their laptops; are they concentrating or goofing around. You must learn to read body language, because this will help you identify, avoid and if necessary react to potential threats.

So, a basic counter-surveillance plan for your home, business or office would be simply to look around the general area and identify where someone could watch you from, then keep an eye on that location from time to time. If someone is hanging around that area take note and if they are there either for an extended time or regularly ask yourself: what are they doing?

Now let's say you have spotted someone acting suspiciously; they are hanging around in a location for too long, for no reason and their body language is not right for the situation, what will you do? If you report suspicious activity to the police then they should send officers to investigate, but in places like the U.S. or Europe where the police have a high work load it can take them time to respond. Or they will not take you seriously as they tend to only respond after a crime has taken place or if there is such thing as a restraining order in place.

You need to work out a plan for what you're going to do if you think you are under surveillance or being stalked, think about who you could call to come and help you, pick you up and take you to a safe location.

I tell my clients to always think like the criminals and put themselves in their shoes; how would YOU watch YOURSELF? How would YOU target YOURSELF? This is a basic threat assessment and something you need to think about on a regular basis as environments and situations change. You can do this with your friends, for example play a game in which you work out how you would kidnap each other... From what you know about each other's routines and lifestyle could you plan a time and location for the crime? Let me give you a hint, check out your friends' Facebook and social media, a lot of people post photos and updates of where they are and what they are doing that can all be used by criminals!

Now, when you are on the streets learn to be aware of your surroundings; when you walk from your office or home be aware of who is around you, weather they are walking, standing around waiting or sitting in a parked car and what's their body language saying? If you are walking to your car check to make sure you are not being followed or if anyone is waiting around your car to ambush you. If you are walking on the street check regularly to make sure you are not being followed; watch for people watching you!

In cities such as London it is common for criminals to identify a victim wearing an expensive watch or jewelry and follow them until they reach a location where they can be robbed. There is a problem in London now with gangs of criminals on scooters and small motorcycles that are robbing people in broad daylight and a lot of times in very nice areas. This happened to a lady I know who was leaving a business meeting in a very nice part of Chelsea; she put her designer handbag in her car and the next thing she knew the car window was smashed by someone riding as a passenger on a motorbike, then another motorbike drove by and the passenger on this one snatched the bag as the driver pointed a gun at her... The whole incident was over in seconds and luckily she was not hurt. She reported the incident to the police and the officer who followed up on the report told her the only reason he was following up was because there was a gun involved, otherwise it was just another robbery. If no one is hurt, it's a low priority crime. Police in London and in a lot of the United Kingdom are under-staffed and underfunded so they do not have the time or resources to deal with a lot of the non-violent crimes.

It's obvious the robbers in this incident were watching the woman, even if only for a short period of time, they were organized and had planned the robbery as the street where it took place had no CCTV cameras. Criminals are constantly looking for victims and planning crimes but very few decent people take precautions and are on the lookout for criminals!

Meetings

Jerry Arrechea is a corporate security manager and world champion martial artist based in Mexico City. Mexico has one of the highest crime rates in the world and is second only to Syria for its murder and violent death rates, so I wanted to know what Jerry recommends to his clients for keeping themselves safe.

"In Mexico we must deal with a wide array of security problems ranging from drug cartel violence to general street crime and there is no magic solution. The criminals here are professionals, they plan and organize their crimes from the initial surveillance of their targets to the escape after the crimes have been committed. It's important for us to be able to identify the criminals in the surveillance and planning stage of their operations and take counter measures. The last thing we want is a confrontation as the criminals are usually very well armed and not afraid to shoot. We would sooner lose goods or money than put our clients in hostile situations.

One situation where we are always extra careful is when we are attending meetings in unfamiliar areas especially with people we don't know 100% as these meetings could be setups for robberies or kidnappings. Before the meeting we do a thorough due diligence check on those we are meeting with, on the day of the meeting we sweep the area looking for any people or vehicles that look suspicious and usually employ protective surveillance personnel while the meeting is taking place to alert us of any suspicious activity that may take place in the area. I advise all my clients, especially females to be cautious when attending meetings where they will be isolated even if they are meeting with people they know to some degree. I have a female self-defense client who is a luxury real estate agent and has had several issues with clients over the years who have tried to sexually assault her while she is showing properties. These days she always has a male driver take her to appointments, has worked out a plan of action if she is attacked and always has something close at hand she can use as a weapon. The last wannabe playboy – someone whom she had met before – who tried to touch her inappropriately ended up with two broken fingers and a broken nose. The only thing left for her driver to do when he came to her assistance was throw the now whimpering playboy off the property....

This lady's driver is a well-trained and dedicated guy, but it still took him time after being alerted to get to her location. She feels it can be intimidating for her clients if she had a bodyguard shadowing her, so her driver usually waits in the car. This is why she had worked out her immediate reaction drill as she knew it would take 15 to 45 seconds for her driver to come to her assistance."

Everyone should think about how they would react to an assault and put a plan in place. Even if you are in an area where the police will come quickly to your assistance, you must know how to alert them if you're in danger and then protect yourself until they are able to reach you. As I said earlier, there is no magic fix, you must be aware of your environment and have plans in place for how to avoid potentially hostile situations and in the worst-case scenarios how to use force to defend yourself!

Street drills

So, you must always be on the lookout for criminals watching you or following you and here I have listed a few simple drills, which are used by professional criminals and security operatives alike. These simple drills will help you identify anyone who is watching or following you. Adapt a few of these drills to your situation, they are simple and proven.

- When walking on the street, turn around and walk back the same way you came; remember the people you walk past or anyone that stops. Also, remember to check on the opposite side of the street for anyone stopping etc. Do this several times and if you see the same person or couples more than once they may be following you.
- If you are driving do a couple of U turns, watch for anyone doing the same and the cars you pass. If you see the same car a couple of times you may be followed.
- Walk around a corner, stop, and remember the first few people that come after you. Again, do this several times and, if you see the same person more than once, they may be following you. Watch the body language of those that come around the corner after you, any flinch could be an indication you have surprised them. You can also do the same when you're driving. From a personal security point remember to always take corners wide as you never know what's waiting for you on the other side.
- Escalators are good for counter-surveillance because whilst ascending you can have a good look around at who is behind you. A simple drill would be to go up and escalator and straight back down again; if anyone is following you they would have to do the same.

- Take special note of people waiting in parked cars, especially near your residence or office. Be especially suspicious of any unattended vans with blacked-out windows parked close to your residence or office. Vans are the most common surveillance and snatch vehicles. As the saying goes, there are only two reasons for two people to be waiting in a car for no apparent reason: they are either having sex or they are on surveillance.
- Go into a café and covertly watch what goes on in the street. Look out for people waiting around to follow you when you leave or anyone who keeps walking past the café, they could be trying to see what you're doing. Pay special attention to locations where people are congregating: bus stops, cafes etc...
- Walk across open spaces such as parks or public squares and see if anyone is running around the outside of the open area trying to keep up with you- they must do this because there is no cover for them in the open space and the distance to go around the open space is greater than walking straight across it.
- Use reflections from windows and other surfaces to see who is behind you or use the selfie camera on your cell phone.
- Try to identify people who look out of place or are waiting in the same place for a long time, such as waiting at a bus stop without getting on any buses or at a payphone for an extended period.
- Be aware of people waiting in a location by themselves, especially fit, young men with short hair. Chances are they are criminals or police. Professional surveillance teams usually consist of mixed couples in their 30's to 50's. Criminals regularly use children, so be wary!
- If you think someone is following you, do not acknowledge them, just slow down and stop to look in shop windows, or go into a café and have a coffee. If you still see the person waiting around, you are most probably under surveillance.
- When you're driving, drive slowly, and take note of anyone doing the same, occasionally pull over and make note of the cars that go past you; if you see the same car more than once you might have a problem.
- If you do not want to look directly at someone who could be following you, look at their feet and remember their shoes. Very few people wear the same shoes, check this out the next time you are out. If you keep seeing the same pair of shoes at various locations, this person could be following you.
- Criminals following you may change their hair, jackets and pants etc. to try and disguise themselves but they rarely change their shoes. The same goes for jewelry or watches, it can be difficult to give a description of someone so look for distinctive jewelry, tattoos or type of cell phone or anything that makes them stand out. If the person is completely non-descript, chances are they are pros.
- If you think someone is following you check their attire to see if they could be concealing cameras or weapons. Are they always on their cell phone possibly

describing your actions or taking photos? What does their body language say, do they look nervous, over observant, are they concentrating too much etc.

- Be suspicious of unknown people who start conversations with you- they could be testing your reactions and personal security level.
- Stop regularly to make telephone calls or look in shop windows as this will allow you to observe your surroundings and identify anyone who may be following you.
- You must make plans on what procedures you will carry out if you are under surveillance. These will depend on where you are and the threat you are under. These days if you think you're being watched, chances are the criminals, terrorists or stalker have already tried to hack your phone or computer, so get them cleaned up and secured!

Now, from a personal security point of view if you are on the street and you seriously think you are being followed get to a safe area as soon as possible and call for someone trusted to come and pick you up. In a lot of countries, you can inform the police, but I strongly expect they won't take the call seriously unless there is a domestic restraining order in place or there is a case history.

If you are being watched, followed or stalked you need to start building up evidence against the criminals or stalker, take videos and write down occurrences. These days most cell phones have cameras and any photos or video you take can be used by the police to identify the suspects and as evidence against them.

Being street wise

Use of force is a last resort and should be avoided at all costs - fighting is for amateurs. You want to do everything possible to identify and avoid any potentially hostile situations. Unlike the movies, street fights are not glamorous, and when guns are involved, people are going to be killed, maimed, or paralyzed. Someone will be going to the hospital or the morgue, and in most places, all those involved will be going to jail.

The bad guys will have put together a mental plan and strategy for robbing or attacking you, so should you not have one for how to counter them? The easiest way to assess someone's personal security is to go up and ask a question like what's the time etc. By doing this and reading their reaction you can tell if the person is security aware or clueless. Now think about how you would react if a stranger approached you and asked you the time; what's your body language going to be saying, are you going to tell them the time, will you be looking at your watch or assessing their body language, will you be in a defensive stance, are you checking for any obstacles in your area that can trip you up, can you access your weapon if you have one?

The criminals want to set you up and catch you off guard. To do this they will use distractions or surprise. If you understand how the criminal operates, you can hopefully spot a potentially hostile situation and avoid it; or if it's unavoidable, reverse the situation so you can escape.

Now from a psychological point of view if someone approaches you and asks you the time and you tell them the time, what have you done? You have complied... So, to help relax you and try to catch you off guard more questions would come, a conversation would be struck up, now you will begin to feel comfortable with the stranger... This is the same tactic that is used for dating and also by sexual predators, I will talk more about this later...

If you have already planned your reaction, you're not going to panic. You'll just be going through your procedures and be setting up the criminal so you can escape or if you're trained to do so you counter attack. So, if a stranger approaches you, start setting them up by assessing their body language, assessing your surroundings, getting yourself into a defensive stance, consider what you want your body language to be saying, identifying your escape routes or as a last resort get ready to use force. You should always use distractions since they can give you the seconds needed to deliver a surprise strike or push that could help you escape.

When you are out and about on your daily business, always consider how you would react if attacked by those around you. The next time you are at the mall or in a coffee shop look around and work out how you could access a weapon, whether you are in a good position, what you could use as cover, and how you would exit the building safely!

As I said earlier, you need to learn how to assess someone's body language and control your own, an important skill since you need to identify someone's intentions and at the same time not to telegraph your potential response.

There are three main components of communication between humans; spoken words contribute 7%, vocal tone and volume make up 38%, and body language makes up 55% of the message. Let's say you're approached by someone while pumping gas in your car, and they are telling you how much they like your car; their breathing rate is shallow and accelerated, they're sweating and making agitated movements with their hands. Are you going to engage them in a conversation about the car or read their body language, assess your surroundings and be ready to run?

To start reading people's body language at a basic level, you can generally tell if people are happy, sad, or angry. Even though it's not 100% reliable, someone's facial expressions are a good indicator of a person's mental state. If stressed, his face will be flushed, perhaps sweating, have veins protruding in neck or forehead and he may be tensing his facial muscles.

When a person is involved in a stressful situation, their body will undergo over 150 different physical stress reactions. These stress reactions will happen to you and criminals alike. You need to be aware of them and be able to notice them in yourself and others. A body's stress reactions include: adrenal surges, increased heart rate and blood circulation, sweating, increased respiration, increased muscular tension, reduced peripheral field of vision, reduced decision-making ability, and reduced hearing capability.

If you have ever been involved in a car accident, try to remember how you felt just before, during, and after. Then try to remember if you felt any of the above reactions. If you have ever tripped over something and subsequently fell, try to remember what it felt like; for example, did the time between you tripping and that of hitting the floor seem longer than the fraction of a second it took in actuality. Were you sweating and was your heart beating rapidly when you hit the floor?

Learn to read your own body language as well as others'. If you are in a situation and your heart rate starts to increase or you start to breathe quickly, try to identify why this is happening. Look for these stress reactions in people around you. If someone approaches you and their face is flushed, eyes are wide and bloodshot, and have veins protruding in their forehead and neck, maybe you want to avoid them or get ready for a confrontation!

Warning signs that identify someone is agitated and a potential threat include direct prolonged eye contact, flushed face, accelerated breathing rate, sweating, veins in neck and forehead protruding, hands moving towards a concealed weapon, hands rising getting ready to strike, eyes narrowing, looking to see if you are armed or at intended target areas on your body, changing to one side for a shooting or fighting stance, and lowering the body before launching an attack.

Always remember, if the criminal is streetwise they will be monitoring your body language and trying to predict your reactions. You should never give any indication that you are going to escape, defend yourself or are armed; your reactions should be a total surprise to your attacker. You must have an offensive mindset, not defensive. You should always keep a low profile, do whatever you can to avoid problems, but if put in a situation where you have to escape or use force, the bad guys will be totally overwhelmed. Remember, fighting is for amateurs – avoid the problems!

This is a short chapter on what is a very important and in-depth subject and I hope it makes you think about your personal security procedures and assists you in putting together a personal security plan. I have not covered self-defense in this handbook as it is a practical skill that needs to be learned from experienced instructors, something you cannot learn from a book. Remember: Ultimately your personal security and the security of your assets is your responsibility!

The security of your home is a main priority but when most people think about this they are only considering the threats from thieves or burglars. Well, there are quite a few other things that you need to consider.

One of the biggest security threats are the people you let into your residence. Now, you should all know that if someone you don't know turns up at your front door not to let them in, even if they claim to be from a utilities company etc. If they don't have an appointment don't open the door and turn them away. If they are persistent then call the police... If someone claiming to be a police officer turns up unexpectedly at your door always verify their identity with their dispatch or station, real cops will understand your concerns!

That young and respectable looking woman knocking on your door could be there to check if anyone is home, to look at your security procedures, if you let her in she will see the layout of your house and if you have anything worth stealing... Think about your procedures for answering the door to a stranger, and ensure your children understand never to open the door to a stranger.

I have had clients who attended my courses and when I asked them how well they knew the cleaners and gardeners they hired the answer was they had no clue who they were. Most seemed to hired from an agency or they were sent by a company and that's fine if the agency or company are vetting their staff properly or, better still, know them personally but many don't.

The domestic help industry is hard work generally poorly paid so it tends to attract those new to a country or those that may have problems obtaining work papers. Now, I am in no way saying that these people are bad, quite the opposite, many times they are dependent on the job and will not do anything stupid to jeopardize it. What I am saying is check to make sure that if they come from a 3rd party they are known and trusted. It's best to always do things by recommendation and check references.

The potential issues that come to most people's minds when letting someone into their home is that they can steal things, which is the obvious one. There is also the issue of people committing illegal activity such as drug use etc. which I will talk about a little later. One potential problem that many ignore is letting visitors use their Wi-Fi and freely giving out passwords. Do you know what these people are searching the web for, if it's child pornography you're going to have a problem. If they are running an internet scam, threatening or blackmailing people all this will come back to your IP address. So, my advice would be try to use parental blocks on your Wi-Fi and change the passwords regularly.

Most people have friends over to visit, many have dinner parties etc. Well, my question is how well do you know your guests? People in general are nosy and many will want to wander through your house, with or without permission. If you don't want people to wander around then lock doors and try to block hallways, pet or child gates attached to an alarm can be a good and affordable deterrent.

One major concern if you have children is when they bring over friends, again do you know their friends, do you know their friends' parents, will they be left unsupervised? Everyone should know the potential issues from leaving teens unattended: sex, drugs, alcohol etc. Now, let me give you some examples of how things can go bad...

- Your teenage son has some friends over and they decide to raid your alcohol cabinet, someone decides to see how much liquor they can drink in one go... Result: A trip to the hospital with a case of alcohol poisoning, which can be fatal.
- Your teenage daughter and her BFF find your prescription medication and decide to experiment, washed down with a little vodka... Result: Depends on the medication but a simple combination of Xanax and alcohol can lead to blackouts, excited delirium or can be fatal.
- You allow your teenage children to have friends over and while you were gone for a short period of time the police received a noise complaint from a neighbor. When the responding officers arrived at your house they smelled the odor of Marijuana, which would be OK if they were over 21 and is a state where it is legal... If not there are going to be problems... Big problems if your house and the teens are searched and quantities over those allowed for personal use or other drugs are found...

Now just from these simple examples we are talking hospitals, fatalities, civil law suits and criminal charges... And let's not forget your children can be taken from you for being a negligent parent. These days small issues can turn into very big problems, very quickly especially where the law and children or teens are concerned.

Prevention is always better than cure and usually a lot cheaper, so take the necessary precautions. Do not leave children unsupervised, educate them to the consequence of potentiality problematic activity, lock up prescription medications and alcohol, search their friends' bags and pockets if they are coming over, talk with their friends' parents about taking precautions. These days if other parents think you are being over cautious they are living in cloud cuckoo land. It takes one mistake to ruin people's lives!

The other issue arising from living not just with children but others in general is people being let into your home without your knowledge. A live-in nanny can sneak her boyfriend in just as your teenage daughter can. I will touch on an issue here that mainly concerns firearms.

I had a client come through my classes who had grown up in a Latin American country where his family owned a farm. One night his father heard a noise in the house, grabbed his legally owned pistol and went to investigate. When he got to the kitchen he bumped into a man in boxer shorts and shot him thinking he was an intruder. Well, the man was the boyfriend of one of the live-in staff and had gone to the kitchen to get something to drink; he was also a police officer. In many places this would have been seen as a justifiable shooting, a genuine mistake but, the country was going communist, land owners were not in favor and the police were not happy one of their own was shot... The father, the shooter was sentenced to prison on a murder charge. He later died in prison...

Every now and again in the US there is a case where a family member shoots another by accident due to mistaking them for an intruder in their homes. If firearms are kept for home security, there must always be good communication between family members as to who is staying in the house and when people are coming and going, there is no room for mistakes and you can't be over cautious.

Residential security

Residential security (RS) is something that is usually taken very lightly, most believe putting in an alarm system and maybe a camera or two is all that's required. The basic procedures I have listed here can be applied to all residences; what will differ is the type and size of the residence and the budget available.

A threat assessment must be compiled, and all vulnerable spots identified. A set of plans needs to be compiled, and procedures drawn up for every eventuality. Now you should search a new property for electronic surveillance devices and contraband such as illegal drugs or weapons that could have been left there by the previous occupants.

If you have children, it pays to search your home on a regular basis for anything they could have brought home, or their friends could have left that could cause problems. The book bag their friend has asked them to look after could contain stolen items, drugs, a firearm etc. Educate your children to the potential risks and take precautions, they may think they are helping someone but in reality, are putting themselves and others at risk.

If the budget allows, alarms and cameras can be installed internally and externally. Always choose the best that you can afford and buy from a reputable dealer; it is best to also get a service agreement and have all equipment regularly serviced by trusted people.

As I have said before, be very careful who you let into your house especially those installing security equipment. Why? Because you want to insure 1. They are installing quality equipment 2. They are placing the cameras in the right areas 3. They are not scoping out your home for their friends to come and rob later 4. They will not be selling or passing on you Wi-Fi, cloud storage and alarm codes to those who will come to rob you later... Get the picture...?

If you move into a house that has cameras installed check to make sure you know the locations of all the cameras and ensure all internet codes are changed, you don't want the previous owners spying on you. Remember if you use internet cameras they can be hacked into, if someone gets access to your computers, smartphones, passwords or on a more professional level access to your server they can also see what you're up to.

Many people have alarm systems and panic buttons in their residences and it amuses me that a lot of people believe that installing an alarm is all it is required to protect their families. We have all seen the commercials on TV where a woman is home alone, the alarm goes off, the bad guy runs away and the alarm company phones her to make sure she is OK; if only the world was that perfect. What if the bad guys aren't worried and expect an alarm to go off because they know they have at least 15 minutes before the police will respond. If you have an alarm system you need to know what the response time will be for those responding, be it an armed response company or the local police.

Another criminal tactic to counter an alarm system in a residence is to keep setting them off until the target turns the system off. Think about it, if over a period of two weeks the alarm on your back door keeps going off between 1am to 4am what would you do? Initially for the first few alarm activations the police will respond, in a lot of places after 3 false alarm activations the police will no longer respond, if you have an armed response company they will be charging you for every alarm they respond to. So, I am sure you will call out the alarm company to fix the alarm, but they will find nothing wrong with it. Would you keep putting up with the cost and aggravation of the apparently false alarm activations or just turn the alarm off? Take nothing at face value, if you have an alarm that starts going off for no apparent reason, look deeper!

Security for a residence needs to be planned in depth with multiple rings of defense, how many you have will depend on the type and size of the residence. When planning the security for a residence you need to think like the criminals. In 1994 I was working in South Africa and was tasked to provide security for numerous residences that had active threats on them. My work day usually started in the early evening and went through to after first light the next morning. When I arrived at a residence the first thing I would do would be to assess the area around the residence for likely criminal surveillance points and approach routes. I would then assess the fence or wall around the garden for the most likely spot the criminals would use as an entry point. I would then take up a position in the garden where I could see the likely criminal entry point or points and as much of the residence as possible, then I waited.

So, the first cordon of security you should consider is the general area around the residence. Consider using CCTV to cover the streets and exterior of the walls of your grounds. If your residence is in an apartment building, the next level of security could take the form of covert CCTV in public areas or placing the building under general protective surveillance. In a large house, this cordon will be the walls or hedges that surround the grounds; these can be monitored by CCTV, with sensors or where legal, topped with razor or electric wire.

In a large residence the next cordon would be the grounds or garden. This area could be covered by CCTV and all external buildings such as garages and tool sheds need to be properly secured. A lot of people ask me about using guard dogs, something I tend to dissuade people from doing. Dogs can be weapons and must be kept under control. In South Africa I had two German Sheppards attack me; they did not die because the client was screaming at me not hurt them. The dogs had been let out of their cage, as they usually were in the evening, by a staff member who did not know I was working there. OK, it was only me, so no problems but what if it was a child or woman and the dogs' owner was not there to take control of them?

If you use dogs they must be properly trained. If I was in a high-risk area would I consider having trained dogs in my garden, sure but they would need to be properly trained. Dogs can be targeted same as security personnel, if they are not trained properly they are easy to poison. Guard dogs that bark a lot are easy to counter, same as an alarm system, we have used this numerous times in parts of Latin America where every house seems to have a pack of dogs, you just need to get the dogs barking and keep them barking, the owner will soon get fed up with it or the dogs will get tired.

The next cordon would be the residence itself, all doors, windows and skylights need to be secured and controlled and if possible, alarmed. Consider defensive gardening to deter criminals gaining access to windows; plant thorny bushes below the window that would make it difficult and noisy for the criminals to get through. Ideally, all rooms should be fitted with motion detectors and in high risk areas locked when not in use.

Now you need to consider what you are going to do if criminals try to make entry to your residence; you need to make plans and preparations for this. In my courses I usually ask people what they would have done if someone tried to break into their house the previous night, a lot of people say they don't know or just then start to think about it. You need to put together sensible procedures, and then if you have an issue you will know what to do and not panic.

There are two general considerations when planning your procedures; are you going to stay in the residence or evacuate, what you do will depend on your situation. A secure room needs to be designated within the residence to be used as a safe room for you and your family in the event of an attack where immediate evacuation is not practical.

The room should be lockable from the inside and have several good communication links with the outside world; there should be a list of emergency numbers in the room, so help can be summoned in the event of an emergency. What equipment is in the room will depend on your situation and the length of time you will need to possible stay in to room, this is where you need to know the approximate response times of those coming to help you. The main thing a safe room needs is an escape route, if I was a criminal and wanted to target someone who I knew took their security serious I would not enter their residence. If someone knows how to defend a building, SWAT and room clearing tactics won't work and you're going to have big problems. The easiest way to clear a building is to cordon it and set it on fire, then attack the inhabitants as they exit.

A set of procedures will need to be drawn up for dealing with visitors to the residence; this is the downfall of most residential security programs. A good example of this happened in Haiti to a business associate of mine and resulted in the kidnapping of family members. This person has a large residence and employed an armed guard to man his front gate. One evening the guard opened the gate to talk with someone who was asking after one of the staff members, as soon as he stepped outside the gate he had a gun put to his head by a criminal who was waiting next to the gate. The criminal with his crew gained access to the residence, as the doors were left open, robbed the place and kidnapped four people.

Also, why should the criminals try to break into a residence when in a lot of cases they can get the occupants to easily open the doors and come to them? As you read this now what would you do if someone crashed into your car; go outside and see what had happened, now you can be kidnapped, and the bad guys have access to your house. A lot of houses have their electric mains outside, same in places where generators are used, so if the criminals cut the power what will most people do; go out and investigate. Sever the connection to most people's satellite TV and what will they do, go outside and check the dish. See the pattern, so do the criminals!

Residential security checklist

Here is list of things you want to consider when planning the security for your residence. Not everything will apply to you but take what does and use it, a lot of the considerations here can be applied to most houses or apartments.

- Always plan security in depth, you want as many cordons of defense as possible.
- Have several means of communications, land-lines and cellular, check them regularly.
- Have planned escape routes.
- If the residence is overlooked, what sniper or surveillance positions are there?
- Check to see if the residence is under surveillance.
- Has the residence been searched for electronic surveillance devices or contraband?

- Is the residence ever left unoccupied, if so it needs to be searched before re-occupation.
- Does the residence have a fence or wall around it and can it realistically keep out intruders?
- Are there gates to the residence, can they stop an intruder or a car, are the gates locked at all times and what are the procedures for greeting visitors.
- Is there anything to help criminals climb over the garden walls or gates, such as trees or poles around the exterior of the property?
- If the residence is in an apartment building, are there fire escapes or scaffolding that could give the criminals a way in?
- Always use counter-surveillance drills before entering and upon exiting the residence.
- What security lights are there, do they work, when are the lights turned on and where is their control switch? If the control switch is outside, move it inside.
- Lights should shine away for the residence not on to it.
- Consider attaching lights triggered by movement detectors outside of doors and vulnerable areas.
- Any defects to floodlighting or other security lights should be fixed ASAP.
- If you are in an apartment building, is the reception manned 24hrs a day and if so, are the people manning it competent? Consider a penetration test.
- Do your doors have peepholes- peepholes are best positioned at the side of the door or in the wall so, you cannot be shot through the door. If using a peephole always extinguish any lights behind you.
- Consider using a video phone to greet visitors and cameras to cover the doors and surrounding areas.
- If you are using guard dogs, make sure they are well trained and preferably under the control of their handler.
- Are all doors to the residence solid and are the doorframes solid, most times a doorframe will break before the lock on the door.
- Are the locks on the doors of a good quality and have you changed them since taking over the residence?
- If a key is lost or an employee fired who has access to keys, change your locks.
- Consider using deadbolts at the top and bottom of a door and wedges in conjunction with the normal locks.
- Can the locks be unlocked from the outside, if a window is broken or can the door hinges be unscrewed?
- Do you have control of all the keys to the residence and have a list of everyone with keys?

- Have all unused entrances and exits secured.
- All windows need to be secured on all floors of the building. It is a fact that in 90% of burglaries, access is gained through windows. Check that windows are properly shut, secured and if possible alarmed.
- Consider putting thorny bushes under windows and around the perimeter of your garden to deter intruders. Thorny bushes can be put on the inside of perimeter walls also to tangle up and alert you to anyone jumping over.
- Beware of casting shadows against windows which can be seen from the outside.
- Consider putting a gravel walkway around the outside of your house so you can hear anyone approaching or stalking around.
- All skylights and roof doors need to be secured and preferably alarmed. Roofs need to be secured and monitored.
- Is the attic of the residence adjoined to another roof or attic from which someone could gain access?
- What alarms are in the residence, are they working and when were they last tested?
- All doors and windows on outbuildings need to be secured, regularly checked and, if possible, alarmed.
- Do all padlocks have spare keys and who has them?
- Are the padlocks of good quality and difficult to pick or shim?
- Are all weapons in the residence legal and are they secured when not in use?
- What firefighting equipment is there in the residence and is it in a serviceable condition?
- Are there any fire alarms and do they work? Fire is the largest cause of loss and damage to private and commercial properties. Fire prevention is, therefore, one of the highest residential security concerns.
- Flooding is a major threat to property and equipment, common causes include taps that have been left running, leaks in plumbing systems or faulty air conditioning systems, heavy rain or snowfall.
- Are all valuables kept secure and do you have pictures of all valuable artwork, jewelry etc.?
- Are all valuables insured and have you recorded the serial numbers of all TVs, computer and stereo equipment?
- Do you, your family and staff have security, emergency procedures and does everyone know them?
- Do you, your family and staff know how to report any suspicious activity in the area?

- Do you, your family and staff know how to the raise the alarm, in the case of an emergency?
- Make arrangements for power cuts, keep spare batteries and bulbs for torches, several means of communications and check them regularly.
- If you have a backup generator, ensure it is serviceable and you have plenty of fuel in a secure location.
- Keep all sensitive and security documentation secure and confidential.
- Keep all medications, prescription drugs and alcohol secured.
- Keep computers and hard drives secure and password protected.
- Have your staff and employees been profiled and had background checks?
- All contractors must have appointments and must be searched before entering and leaving the residence. Searched when entering to check for contraband and when leaving to make sure they are not stealing anything.
- Contractors should always be accompanied.
- If suspicious of visitors, turn them away or keep them outside and preferably illuminated, until their credentials are verified. Also consider that they could be testing your security or a distraction while others try to access your residence.
- Never illuminate yourself in a doorway or a window, darkness is your friend.
- Use a mailbox or virtual office address rather than your residential address.
- Be suspicious of unexpected power outages, faulty alarms etc.
- Always have escape routes and don't let security procedures obstruct them.
- Know the location and safest routes to safe houses, emergency rendezvous points, hospitals, etc.
- Think like a criminal and plan for every eventuality.

School security can be a challenging problem for parents and children alike and there is a wide array of potential problems ranging from active shooters, gang activity, bullying and sexual predators.

Sadly, most parents have little say in the overall security of school facilities and have to leave this to the school's boards, heads and local policies. They can voice their concerns but to get things changed depends on politics, budgets, resources and dealing with the egos of those perfect people in charge that cannot take constructive criticism.

I am sure most schools and their staff are very concerned about the safety and wellbeing of their students but as I have said are restricted on what they can do due to budgets and resources. Sadly, we have recently seen at the school shooting in Parkland Florida a police officer assigned to the school who hid and did not confront the shooter, which many believe lead to the deaths of multiple children.

This highlights a basic security principle and truth that I convey to my clients and students... Your personal security is your responsibility, never expect others to inconvenience or put themselves in harm's way for you! Now, from what I understand about the Parkland incident there were MANY police and Fire Rescue/Para-Medics who wanted to enter the school but were told to stand down by their command... This is an example of what can be expected in such a situation, chaos...

Consequently, how can you - as a parent - protect you child in such situations where you will not be with them? Firstly, assess the school's security and raise any concerns you have with the school authorities in writing. Find out what the school's procedures are for active shooter situations then sit down with your children and ensure they know what to do if an incident occurs during class or while they are on break. I go into a lot more details on active shooter situations in my other book "Counter Terrorism: IED/Bomb & Active Shooter Response". Sadly, this is an issue that nowadays everyone needs to be aware of and educated on.

Social Issues

A lot of the problems and pressures a child faces at school are form other students; children like to tease and make fun of others, that's a fact of life. How other children respond can lead to situations escalating or de-escalating. A common saying when I was a child was "Sticks and stones may break my bones, but words will never hurt me", which is very true.

When serving in the British Army (Infantry) we were constantly looking for reasons to humiliate, play extreme pranks and jokes on each other... And I mean extreme... The only way to counter such incidents is laugh along with them, not to let them bother you, if it was seen you were getting upset or aggravated then the games would continue.

So, the best defense against teasing is to ignore, if others don't like you then that's their problem, avoid and focus on your positive goals and friends. Things can get trickier when the teasing turns to physical bullying. Back in the day children were told if they were hit and bullied to hit back, well in today's world that can lead to them being arrested. I left school over 30 years ago in the UK and I cannot remember once when the police came to the school because of kids fighting. From what I see and understand in the US these days if children of whatever age get into a fight the police are called, which in my opinion is extreme and more than a little crazy. I take it the kids are then sent to counseling, put on medications and then go on to suffer from anxiety and depression... I think the old ways worked a lot better!

If your child is being bullied it can be a challenge to deal with these days, sending them to boxing classes can result in them having more problems but I would send them anyway. A lot of the issues that come from bullying are not just physical but psychological so, any activities that will boost your child's confidence and self-esteem are a must to counter any negatives. If you choose to send them for self-defense classes they must understand that the use of force is a last resort and they must do everything to avoid confrontations.

From a parent's point of view if your child is being bullied it's a situation that needs to be managed. For the school authorities or police to take any complains seriously you need to present evidence such as who the bullies are, when and where incidents took place, what happened, what was stolen or what injuries your child suffered. Go over things with your child and let them know you support them and work out a plan together. If the bullying is serious and constant you should take to school the evidence you have and try to get those responsible disciplined or your child moved to another class or school.

Gangs

It's human nature for people to want to identify and belong to certain social groups, such things as sports teams are a positive on the other hand gangs are negative. Children and teens are drawn to them for various reasons, they are seeking acceptance, social status, peer-pressure or they see it as a potential to make quick money when in reality these things are short lived, and most gangbangers end up in jail pretty quickly.

When looking at a child's motivations think back to when you were that age, what were your priorities, and did you understand the big picture of how the world worked? I doubt you did, and the decisions you made between the ages of 13 to 16 affected your future. If a teenage makes the wrong decisions these days their life can be ruined.

Most gang culture requires initiations which usually involve violence or crime, so to start with the potential gang members can end up in serious trouble before they are even really started. In the gang mentality trouble is good, if you are arrested or jailed it adds to your gang credibility. The rest of the world views it as screw ups but in their gang world it's expected behavior. Sadly, it takes most gang members, the ones that live, quite a few years to realize they have wasted their lives. By which time due to their criminal records they struggle to even get an OK job let alone a serious career.

It's very sad the main stream culture glamorizes gangsters and narcos from Rap Music to the Sopranos and the Godfather movies, the reality is far different. How many Rappers have been shot and killed, how many narcos are killed daily in Mexico, how many narco bosses are in jail, even Pablo Escobar was killed by security forces and John Gotti died in prison, glamourous right!

For a parent it is essential you are aware and know your child's friends and who they are socializing with and where. It's very easy for a child to get caught up with the wrong crowd and be in a world of trouble very quickly. You need to educate your children on the issues of gang membership and if you believe they are heading in that direction you need to act quickly to correct their behavior. My advice would be if a kid wants to be a tough guy let them, sign them up for boxing or MMA classes with a disciplined and credible gym, push them to join military cadets, youth or teen program, in addition to being challenged they will also find a positive group to identify with. Every parent needs to be looking for indicators of gang membership, below is a list of main changes in behavior that should raise concerns.

- They start to socialize with known troublemakers or gang members
- They start to wear or want buy clothes of particular colors or with a specific logo
- They start to wear dark or black clothing when they go out at night
- They start to wear hoodies, bandannas and ball caps that shield their face
- They use hand signs when greeting, talking with or leaving friends
- The start to use a new nickname and even ask family to use it
- They start to follow a specific type of music
- They have graffiti, specific signs or symbols drawn on their possessions
- They have specific signs or symbols tattooed or cut on them
- They start to get into fights or come home bruised or cut and refuse to explain what happened
- They start to speak in a slang or use curse words regularly
- They withdraw from interacting with family members and seek privacy when not with their friends
- They lose interest in their old hobbies and activities
- They start to have an aggressive and over confident attitude
- They start to get into trouble, skipping school and staying out late
- They start to have unexplained cash, jewelry, phones and items that are beyond their allowance or what they earn
- They start to show signs of drug use and possess drug paraphernalia
- They start to buy and carry weapons
- They get into trouble or are spoken to by the police

Now if you identify some of these indicators then you need to take action, which can be very difficult. These days most schools and police departments have programs that can help, remember taking things into your own hands these days can get you into a lot of trouble... The child who wants to be a gangbanger can quickly resort to being sweet and innocent when they call the police on you for threatening to give a spanking. So, be aware of what you can do legally, if you're taken to jail you won't be setting a good example...

ONLINE SECURITY

These days the majority of people use some type of social media platform for business, to stay in touch with friends, dating or virtual socializing. Social media can be both a positive and negative influence in people's lives, it's up to you which it is.

The golden rule with anything you do online is never post information that you don't want made public or others to know about. All social media platforms have some type of privacy setting which you need to review before using but remember anything online can be hacked.

There are regularly stories in the media about large corporations etc. having their systems hacked and losing data and they have full time, skilled cyber security departments. I doubt you have the budget to employ a squad of cyber geeks so, you need to be your own online security expert and if you follow some basic rules you should be able to keep yourself safe...

One of the largest hacks of a dating site was that of "Ashley Madison", a site dedicated to hookups for married people looking for extra-marital affairs. I am sure a lot of people had problems due to this hack, not only marital problems but also a lot of embarrassment. As I have already said, never post or do anything online you don't want others to know about or could expose you to being blackmailed. I will talk more about this and sexual predators in the next chapter.

Everyone should know these days never to give out personal information online, especially financial information to anyone you don't know. Even if you know someone it is far safer passing over sensitive information face-to-face, if you must do it via the internet or smartphone split the information via two platforms for example username via Facebook & password via Instagram etc.

If someone you don't know approaches you online, treat them like a stranger as you would someone turning up at your front door. By letting someone into your social media world you are really letting them into your home, you are giving them access to your personal world. So, be careful who you let in, what information you give them and where you let them go.

If a stranger wants to join your social media network check them out, if they are connected with your other contacts ask them if they know this person. See if their profiles actually look real or are fake. Indicators of fake profiles are that they are new, have few photos, posts, friends... I regularly get friend requests on Facebook from women I have never met, usually a sexy chick with a new profile, a few revealing pics, no friends or a lot of male friends, all red flags indicating a scammer. Don't be worried about deleting someone's request, remember it's your personal space.

A while ago someone I know, dislike and would never trust was trying to access one of my personal Facebook accounts by sending friend requests from fake accounts portraying attractive women from various locations I have lived in. I take it this guy wanted access to my Facebook account to look for business contacts. One of the red flags pointing to the suspicious guy was when someone contacted me asking if he had worked for me in Haiti, of course he had never worked for me or my companies and was just a wannabe I bumped into over the years...

I have a friend whose banking info was stolen recently. Thankfully he spotted the problem quickly and alerted his bank and changed his passwords. He thinks the attack came from a text message he received from a stranger which contained a web link he opened only to find it led nowhere but gave the criminals access to his phone.

Spyware is widely available and easy to install on smartphones via someone having physical access to your phone or by sending you an attachment or link to open. Commercial spyware is generally marketed so you can monitor your children's or employee's activities but can also be used by stalkers or private investigators etc. to monitor your movements, messages, calls and online activity. One recommended way to clear spyware from your phone is to reset it to the factory settings and clear out all the apps and data or get a new phone!

I had one client contact me a few years ago with a stalker problem; for this lady if was more of a case of an annoying stalker that kept turning up when she was out to dinner or socializing. Luckily, the guy didn't have any violent tendencies, and was just seeking attention. The lady could not figure out how this guy always knew her whereabouts and believed he had her under some high-tech surveillance, when in reality she had all of here social media settings set to "Public". She was one of those people who post their comings and goings, what they are eating or drinking, where they are and with whom and all this was open for everyone to see.

If you're someone who likes to post your life on social media, ensure your privacy setting are set correctly and you only let trusted people in your network and even then, remember these trusted people could also be passing your postings on to others. If you are concerned about people knowing your location but want people to know you were at a certain place, consider delaying posting until after you have left the location.

By posting your location you are also letting others know you are not home, an ideal thing for burglars. If you are a parent, make sure your children know not to post such things as when they are home alone or have a non-adult babysitter minding them as this can be an open invitation for sexual predators to pay a visit.

Children's phones and computers need to be monitored and parental blocks used to stop them from using inappropriate sites or apps. Also, you need to monitor their chats and messages with their friends to ensure they are not getting up to things they should not. I have encountered parents who were worried about offending their teens by monitoring their social media accounts... Well 1. Who's paying the bills and 2. It's better to offend them than bail them out from jail, go visit them at the hospital or identify their body at the morgue... Just saying!

These days in many places complaints about social media postings make up a major part of the complaints received by police. A lot of which are nothing more than BS which wastes police time and resources. Saying that, a lot of problems, especially gang related violence stem for what has been said and posted on social media platforms.

I am sure all of us can say that we have seen something online that we don't agree with or someone has sent us an abusive message at some point, well the beauty of the virtual reality world is that you can delete the message, block the sender and move on. If this happens to be someone you work with or go to school with then keep a distance from them in the real world as well. Who you let into your world is your choice, only let in those who are positive for you.

Do not get into online arguments with people and start being abusive as this can end up getting you into trouble, even if you are just responding to someone else's abuse. These days a simple insult can be turned against you, so it is better -as I just said- to delete, block and ignore the other person.

If you or your child is being cyber stalked, bullied or threatened then you should keep all the messages sent to you and all other activity that if necessary can be used as evidence if the situation gets to the point where you need to inform the authorities. So, to finish up I will say again, your online "virtual" world is still your world and personal space so, it's up to you who you let in!

Online security tips

- Set strong passwords for your phones and computers
- Set different password for all of your social media accounts.
- Use the two-factor authentication option that is available for most social media platforms.
- Don't give out your usernames and passwords or write them down where they can be read by others.
- Be very selective with friend requests and who you let on your social media accounts.
- If you don't know the person who sent the request, don't approve them, it could be the fake account of a scammer, stalker or sexual predator.
- If you are sent links or downloads by a friend always confirm they really sent them, their accounts could have been hacked and the link will download a Trojan virus.
- Be careful about what you post online. Don't post anything you do not want to be made public. Such things as posting your home address, financial information, phone number can lead to identity theft just to start with.
- Never post your location in real time as potential stalkers know where you are and burglars know you're not home.
- Learn the privacy settings of the social media platforms you use and customize them for your requirements.
- Do not use your personal accounts for business or virtual socializing.
- Keep your software up to date and use decent antivirus software.
- Always remember to log off especially if others have access to the computer or phone you were using.

SEXTING & SEXTORTION

Sexting and sextortion are issues that have developed with the prevalence of camera phones and the internet, so they are relatively modern problems.

Sexting is simply where people send each other revealing, naked or sexually explicit photos, which is OK between trusting couples if they are of the legal age to do so, but remember what I have said previously, everything you put online, send over the internet, store on your phone can be made public.

Even if the photos and videos are sent between trusting couples they can still end up in the public domain as social media accounts can be hacked, phones stolen or lost, the images can be sent to the wrong people etc.

One of the major problems with sexting is that people will share the photos with their friends, who will in turn share the photo, so your naked selfies can end up going viral and global.

There have been many suicides related to sexting, usually where a teenager's naked images are sent to their supposed boyfriend or girlfriend who then goes and spams them out to all their school friends etc. There have been incidents where teenage boys are competing amongst themselves by setting up private Instagram accounts just to post reveling or sexual photos they have managed to obtain from unsuspecting girls.

Teenagers do such things, and this is another reason why parents must monitor their child's social media and messengers. What a teenager can deem as just some fun in reality can cause them major embarrassments and at that age can affect them psychologically. There is also the very real problem of your child being groomed by pedophiles, which can open the door to your child being set up to be sexually abused.

The laws on the age when someone can engage in consensual sex vary from country to country but be assured if someone under the legal age of consent sends an older person indecent images it will be classed as child pornography. For example, if your teen has a younger girlfriend, there could be a problem in some locations when he turns 18 years old and has a naked picture of his 17-year-old girlfriend on his phone... As parents you need to be aware of what your children are doing and also the laws that could affect them, again this is about educating people to avoid potential problems.

Revenge porn can apply to people of all ages who have been sending out naked photos or been videoed having sex. Revenge porn occurs when an ex-boy or girlfriend posts sexual images online to embarrass or get revenge on their ex-partner. In many places now revenge porn is a crime, but those posting the images and videos are now getting away with the crime by simply stating it was not revenge, it was consensual, and the other person wanted their sex videos online, which some people do.

If someone does engage in revenge porn and posts a sexual video of their ex-partner or someone they picked up in a bar, you would have to prove it was them who posted the videos in order to get the person charged by the police They could have shared the videos with friends who then posted or sold the videos to a porn site. Now things would have gotten very complicated legally and in the meantime your sex tapes and photos could be viewed by millions of perverts globally.

Sextortion

Sextortion is a crime they are having big problems with in Europe. An old friend of mine from the British Army who is now a British Police Detective was explaining they are receiving a lot of calls from people who have been caught out by this scam.

This is how things usually develop: the scammer will set up a social media profile of an attractive young girl or boy and then start sending out friend requests to likely looking victims. When someone accepts their friend request they start to politely message then build up a virtual relationship over say a few weeks. When they feel the victim is comfortable with them they start sending nude and sexual photos or videos and asking the same in return.

When the scammers have sufficient videos and photos of the victim then the extortion begins. The threat is usually for a relatively small amount of money, £250.00 GBP; why so small, because this is an amount most can afford however it is a lot of money in Nigeria. If the victim refuses to pay, then the scammers tell them that they have or had access to their friends and contacts list and will send their sexual photos or videos out to everyone.

For most people this would cause a lot of embarrassment, for those with work colleagues, bosses or employers on their social media it could cost them their job. I am quite sure the vast majority of these cases are not reported to the police and the victims pay up.

This scam is also very prevalent in the Middle East and Central Asia where the cultures are very conservative. The scammers target these cultures because they know if they make public a sexually explicit video of someone from Saudi Arabia for example, that person could end up in a lot of legal problems. In many Central Asian cultures, it would lead to the person being disowned by their family or in the case of a female, an honor killing.

So, while sexting can appear to be just harmless fun it can generate a lot of negative repercussions ranging from embarrassment, loss of friends, law suits, criminal complaints, extortion and suicides. How can all this be prevented? Very simply... Do not let people you don't know or trust into your social media networks and if you need to let work colleagues or others whom you don't know, or trust then be careful what you post and set another personal profile for close friends. Also, the golden rule, do not send or post anything that you are not comfortable with being made public!

SEXUAL PREDATORS

Now this is a chapter everyone must read, especially if you're a parent, the threat from sexual predators is very, very real whoever you are and wherever you are.

Regularly there are stories in the media of men in influential positions who have used their influence and connections to facilitate and cover up sexual assaults on women, men and children. This is something that has been going on since the beginning of time, but due to today's awareness of such crimes and the ability for them to be easily reported to police it is making life a lot harder for the predators and more difficult to stay under the radar.

Sexual predators come from all walks of life be it the politician, the Hollywood film producer, the local priest, the school teacher or the apparently nice man that hangs around the children's play area at your local park. You must always be assessing others and questioning their motivations, some of you may say this is extreme and paranoid, which is fine by me, ultimately your personal safety and that of your family are none of my business, I write, I advise and thank you for reading my work... Hopefully you won't be reading about yourself or your family in one of my future articles or books, if you are then thank you for giving me the content!

Now a lady I know well told me about an incident that happened to her recently that caught her off guard. To start with she is a well-traveled woman and a lot sharper than most... She needed to pick up some documents from an associate of hers, so they agreed to meet half way. That day a bad South Florida thunder storm had caused a power outage at her home and she took her phone charger with her as the battery was low.

She was going to meet her associate at a "Krispy Kreme" coffee and doughnut shop just off I-95, a main highway in suburban South Florida. The lady was dressed very casually as she had rushed out and when she got to the coffee shop she grabbed a coffee, sat at a table and plugged in her phone to charge.

After being there a few minutes a well-dressed, well-spoken man approached her, and started to make small talk, she engaged him politely. She remembers saying something about being glad to be able to charge the phone since there was no power at home and the man responded by offering to pay her phone and electricity bills if she would come back to his hotel with him... Caught off balance, she explained she had no power due an outage and she could pay her own bills, thank you... The man left...

This was the classic behavior of a sexual predator who had most probably done this many times before. He chose the location, a coffee shop off a major highway, because this would be a place where vagrants, hitchhikers and those traveling would hangout looking for a ride. The fact the lady was dressed down, by herself and charging her phone made her fit his profile of a victim... Someone in need... The fact he left straight away after being rebuffed means he was wise enough to leave before the police were possibly called.

When the lady spoke to me about the incident things were still sinking in and she was shocked and bewildered. Now she understands the true nature of this encounter and it's opened her eyes to a world she never knew existed...

Many a time I've seen parents drop off their teenage children to do their homework together or socialize at Starbucks Coffee shops in my local area. Starbucks has free Wi-Fi, is usually clean and attracts a mix of professional and student types as clientele, so it's an apparently safe environment. What I have noticed on several occasions is older men who will go out of their way to approach girls in school uniforms to strike up a conversation... To me, this is odd as there are usually plenty of others to talk to, in their age range and younger, usually an attractive woman or two sitting alone or with friends... So, why approach these school girls? All I can say is if those were my daughters I would be concerned about the men's motives.

Even in such apparently safe environments you must educate your children what to do if they are approached by a stranger, the men could be asking an honest question, or they could be trying to open an opportunity for grooming. Your children should know to never give their contact details to strangers be it phone numbers or Facebook profile addresses etc. They also have to be careful who is watching them and who can see what they are looking at on their computers or phones. Just by sitting behind someone who is on their computer in a coffee shop you can see who they are talking to and the details of their social media profiles. A pedophile only needs the name on your child's Facebook account to be able to start trying to make contact and start grooming.

If they are being pestered or harassed by someone they should know to call or message you or report the person to the staff at the location they are in. They should never leave the location or go to the bathroom alone if they are uncomfortable with someone watching them or acting strangely. Again, this is basic common sense, but children need to be made aware!

In the 1990's when I was working in London the hotels always had a problem with perverts and sexual predators cruising for victims and using the toilets that were open to the public as places to have sex. One hotel in particular, just off Piccadilly Circus, was renowned as pick up location for rent boys (male prostitutes). I have too many stories from my time in London working as a freelance bouncer, hotel & VIP event security and bodyguard but I chose a couple of incidents from that hotel and will high-light a few things for you to consider.

I remember one incident where my colleague and I spotted some kids, two boys and a girl, in the games room, with beer bottles on their table. They must have been in their early teens and clearly well under the legal drinking age. The girl was the oldest of the group, maybe 14 and wearing a lot of makeup... When we approached them a man whom we did not see as he was slouching in a chair behind them told us they were OK as they were with him... OK, but he was drunk, he had a British accent and the kids were German, they were staying in the hotel and he was not... And let's not forget they had beers in front of them...

To make a long story short, the man was detained, and the kids' parents located. When the man realized the police had been called he needed to be restrained, after the police arrived, took him to hospital and worked out his identity, they called us back to let us know he had arrest warrants and we should not be seeing him for a while. In the meantime, the kids' parents were in disbelief as to what had just happened, they had been in a coffee shop outside the games room, in the hotel foyer, they though their kids were safe and just playing the video games, they also did not realize the games room had an entrance from the street.

One of the big problems with that hotel, as there is with many, was poor management and the focus being on filling rooms with little consideration for guest security. I was freelance working on an as needed basis, so their policies and procedures were not my concern or business. I remember being there several times when they had large school groups in residence, I am talking pre-teens and early teens, and instead of having them in adjoining rooms on the same floor they had them spread out throughout the hotel. The hotel at that time had no en-suite bathrooms just communal ones at the ends of the hallways. So, there was an issue with children wandering around the corridors at all hours looking either for the bathrooms or their friends.

You cannot blame the kids' teachers or the trip organizers for the risks to the children, instead of rooms being set aside for them the booking staff had just assigned them what rooms they had available when they turned up. The teachers did not realize the situation until they arrived, until security contacted them with a request to tell the children not to wander around the floors, not to answer the doors to strangers etc. because they were in "pervert central". Of course, the security team was never informed of school group arrivals and our first indicator was unattended children wandering around... So, if you're a parent and your kids are going on a school trip make sure you do your research on where they are staying and ensure nothing is left to chance!

I can say from my experience of dealing with London's perverts, freaks and hookers that many do not fit the stereotype. Quite a few times did we have to escort the tweed jacketed country gents or the sharp suited city gents from a hotel or event due to their highly questionable behavior, usually in the public restrooms... So, never let someone's appearance and social status deceive you to their intentions.

I always tell my clients never allow yourself to be put in a situation where you can be taken advantage of, assaulted physically or raped. Also, never allow others to put you in such a situation...

One story that comes to mind is of another lady I know who is an artist and was put in a very questionable situation while trying to repossess some of her art work from an art dealer. She had given this art dealer over $100K's worth of art to sell for a $15k retainer. When the dealer was not selling the pieces, the artist wanted the works back and the BS began.

The artist whom I have known for years had already complained the art dealer had made inappropriate sexual advances towards her but being a former professional model, she put it down as being part of doing business with wealthy older men. Anyway, she managed to strike an agreement with the art dealer via a Florida attorney friend of his who was just as sleazy...

When the time came for her to go pick up the paintings from the home of the art dealer in the suburbs of Atlanta, Georgia she asked me to go with her as she was not comfortable with the situations and rightly so. The pickup had been arranged by the Florida attorney and neither he nor the art dealer knew she was taking me with her. When we arrived at the dealer's house it was clear that he and his helper were surprised and not particularly happy to see that the artist had brought me along.

Even though the pickup had been arranged for days none of the paintings had been taken out of the house or prepared for the move. Anyhow, the paintings were loaded into our van and we left, job done.

Now, was that a situation, with the known background, a situation where this lady should have gone by herself... NO WAY! She would have been in an isolated area, with a man who had made sexual advances towards her and who she was now in a business dispute with. Why the paintings were not ready to move and what the art dealer's intentions were for that day, who knows, maybe my opinion of humanity in general is very low but it's not usually wrong...

So, never put yourself in situations where you will be vulnerable, never put yourself in situations with people you are uncomfortable with, never put yourself in situations where you could be raped or sexually assaulted and this applies to everyone, male and female. Parents must always know where their children are and who they are with and they should only be left alone with those you can trust with your own life!

Child grooming

Another form of behavior by sexual predators that parents need to be aware of is Child Grooming, this problem has become more prevalent as the internet and social media applications have become freely available to people of all ages. Child grooming is where a sexual predator will befriend a child and sometimes even the child's family with the intent to exploit the child for sexual purposes. The child can be exploited to perform sexual acts, provide sexual photos or videos or used for prostitution and trafficked.

Child groomers aim to get the trust of the child and their families to be able to get time alone with their victims. A child stating that a close family friend or person in authority has been talking to them about sexual matters, giving them gifts or seeking to spend time alone with them could be a red light that something is not right.

Internet child groomers often set up social media profiles pretending to be a child the same age as the ones they are looking to victimize. They shower their victims with compliments and gifts and seek sexual photos, videos and possible meetings in return. Young girls are the main target of internet groomers, but boys are also targeted, with most activity happening via smart phones, children with attention seeking behavioral issues are most at risk. This is where parents must monitor their child's phones, computers and read the messages they are sending their friends. Why, because the Facebook profile that portrays a teenage girl the same age as your daughter could be a much older sexual predator trying to get her to send them indecent images.

In the United Kingdom there have been several high-profile cases where immigrant gangs from central Asia have targeted underage girls from broken homes and dysfunctional families. Sexual predators tend to pray on vulnerable people, they disguise their perverted intentions as bogus acts of kindness. The girls were provided with alcohol and drugs and then exploited for sexual purposes and prostitution. These girls were targeted because they came from troubled backgrounds and were already vulnerable, had care givers that did not care about them and were easy to befriend and exploit. People who have suffered neglect or are going through problems, especially children, respond to acts of kindness, because they are not use to that and when people are kind to them they bond to these people.

Parents must monitor their children, who are they meeting or socializing with and where they are at all times. Children and teenagers' phones and computers must be monitored, again, what could appear to be an innocent friend request on a social media application could just as easily be an approach by a sexual predator. Monitor all their messages, even to those responsible adults that you know and trust, if the adults find out and are offended, I would question their friendship.

Child kidnapping & slavery

Every parent's worst nightmare is that their child will go missing and be returned harmed or will just never be seen again. Parents must know where their children are always! In a later chapter I will talk about domestic child kidnapping and child kidnapping prevention, here I want to highlight the issues from sexual predators.

At the time of writing this I have just been approached by a non-profit organization that is looking for a missing girl, well a 20-year-old young woman. The girl was last seen out with friends at a bar from where she left drunk, some report she had been drinking heavily, some believe her drink had been drugged, anyway that was the last she was ever seen. The local police have left the case open and done all the follow up's they possible could, but she disappeared.

Without going into details a few years after she vanished, a photo was recovered from a computer during a police raid on a pedophile's home that showed what appeared to be the missing girl in a very bad condition and the photo was traced to another country. Speculation is she was kidnapped specifically to be trafficked and sold or possibly set up to be kidnapped to pay off someone's drug debts.

Children, teens and young people being kidnapped and sold for sexual slavery is a very real issue. There are criminal networks that specialize in selling people for sexual slavery. They tend to target those people who, if they disappear, no one will notice or care; illegal immigrants, the homeless, drug addicts or those already working as prostitutes. So, with an already large supply of victims why target and kidnap someone from the "Normal" world? Well, because they can be worth a lot more money.

The problem is when teens and young adults go missing who's to say they have not just left home, ran away or are off partying with friends. So, any police response can be delayed unless there is hard evidence of a kidnapping. By which time the victim can be in another country or long deceased.

As a parent and guardian, you must ensure your children are aware of the threat and again know where they are and what they are doing to the best of your ability, which can be difficult with teens and young adults. I think all involved in this case of the missing girl have accepted the she is dead, and I expect she died in an extreme manner. I don't know if I can say if she is lucky enough to still be alive, but I will say if she is still alive she is most likely a strung-out junkie somewhere...

Now, so far, I have only spoken of men being sexual predators, but women are also responsible for using children, teens and young adults for sexual exploitations. Women are usually the accomplices and help groom those being targeted for sexual abuse, prostitution or trafficking. Most people will not suspect a woman of doing such awful things but there are almost always women involved in grooming and trafficking gangs.

For another insight into the issue of child kidnapping I reached out to a friend and professional investigator who has and dealt with cases concerning children being trafficked for use in Black Magic rituals. Dimitris K of Risks Incorporated has a religious background and over the years has conducted investigations into occult activity in Europe. I asked him his opinions on today's problems with child grooming and kidnapping.

Dimitris stated: "In Europe now the problem with sexual predators is extremely high, not only are we talking about children being groomed online but also the threat of children being abused and kidnapped off the street. The refugee epidemic in Europe means no-one knows who is in their countries... Sexual predators are undocumented, the children they pray on are undocumented."

"The undocumented children are prime targets for pedophiles and trafficking gangs that will groom them or just kidnap them and then sell them for prostitution and pornography. As you well know, there have been numerous cases where children have been trafficked, used and sacrificed for occult ceremonies, this is a reality and sadly something I expect we will see more of in the future."

"From our experience and research, we know that sexual predators and occult practitioners come from all walks of life and can be found everywhere. They go out of their way to disguise themselves as the perfect citizens, so their illicit activities will not be expected. "

"In March this year (2018) the Spanish Police while working with the Nigerian Police and British National Crime Agency broke up a large gang of human traffickers and made I believe over 80 arrests. These Nigerian traffickers are using black magic as an intimidator to make these women and girls comply with their demands and force them into prostitution. A lot of those men that go on to abuse these women and girls are outwardly respectable people, but under their fine suits they are depraved animals.

"I am a father and will always watch over my children, I know where they always are and who they are with. I make a point of knowing their friends, and their friends' families, it's my duty to do so. I do not spy on my children, I do not have to, we have an agreement that I can check their social media accounts and they will tell me if some stranger approaches them online or in person. These days we must be this way and the children must understand we are working as a team, as a family. And this is the approach I would recommend to every parent, wherever they are living!"

Dimitris' advice is basic and common sense and should be applied by all parents, having good communications with your children is essential. Following is a list of possible indicators that a child is being groomed or sexually abused, this is not a definitive list, it's just a guide to possible indicators.

- The child has difficulty walking, sitting or reports unusual pain or injuries to their private areas
- The child refuses to change for gym or to participate in physical activities

- The child reports having nightmares or bedwetting
- The child is nervous and reluctant to be left alone with adults
- The child's stops eating regularly
- The child has advanced sexual knowledge and behavior
- The child reports receiving gifts or money from non-immediate family or strangers
- The child is isolated and spends a lot of time on the internet or on their smart phone
- The child is secretive and will not allow the parent access to their phone or computer
- The child is very comfortable around adult strangers
- The child runs away from home, self-harms or attempts suicide
- The child is in possession of condoms or contraception, gets pregnant or contracts venereal diseases
- The child reports being sexually abused
- The child's parent or care giver keeps the child isolated
- The child's parent or care giver is over protective of the child
- The child's parent or care giver is jealous or controlling with family members as far as access to the child is concerned.

If anyone has been a victim of a sexual assault the police need to be informed, in many places if a child has been assaulted and you know about it and don't report it, it makes you an accomplice in the case and criminally liable. If you believe a child is being groomed or sexually abused, you must inform the police immediately. Virtually all police departments have specially trained officers and support staff to deal with sex crimes and the victims.

Hopefully from this chapter you can see the threat from sexual predators is very real and something that can be encountered by everyone. Education is your best defense, educate yourself and your children to do everything possible to avoid sexual predators and potentially hostile situations.

DATING

Dating is a topic that can apply to parents and children alike, many parents get divorced or are single for multiple reasons. So most parents should be able to relate to what I talk about in this chapter, if not from their own experience then from that of their friends.

I have been thinking for a few months on how to structure this chapter as this is a very complicated subject and as usual, I have loads of stories of my own and others, adventures and misadventures, some of which I want to include to highlight certain situations. I will focus on the very basics of dating emphasizing problems that can occur and what people should be aware of. I intend to be very blunt in this chapter because dating and relationships is a main area in most people's lives that seems to generate the most problems.

I think every adult has had problems with dating, some of us learn from our experience but many don't. I think one of the main problems with people and relationships is that people seem to feel they must be dating someone or there is something wrong with them. In my opinion this has more to do with social pressure than what is good for the person. If you are having to work hard to get into and keep relationships going, then I don't think they are meant to be. People need to fit easily into your life, you shouldn't have to restructure yours for them, and if you do chances are you will only end up resentful and unhappy.

Those of us who are parents must remember your choices also affect your children, so you must make them carefully, what you bring into your life is also coming into your child's life. These days there are so many wackos out there and you do not want to accidentally end up introducing your children to drug users, psychos, domestic abusers or pedophiles!

The beginnings

From the start off, relationships can pose a multitude of security related issues and you must be very careful how you approach things. The issue with meeting new people is that you don't really know who they are, especially when dating.

The aim of dating is to try to impress someone else so people will over exaggerate everything about themselves and lie about all sorts of things from age to income and marital status. I am sure all the adults reading this have some personal experience or have heard stories from their friends about dating people who start out seemingly as the ideal partner only to later reveal themselves as a fraud and a phony.

Many relationships start online these days via social media or dating sites which can be a security risk but can also be a security aid. As with anything online you must remember it truly is a virtual reality where you can portray yourself as anyone you want, you can create whatever life story you want and many do so for multiple reasons. This is where you will have to try and figure out if the other person is real or just trying to impress and manipulate you into sending them naked selfies.

The benefits of online dating for the wise is that you screen people before you meet them to try to identify any potential issues and at least work out if they are compatible for a coffee date at least. Always try to cross reference any of their claims by running an online check on their name to see what pops up, verify any company they claim to work for, try to obtain a current photo so you know what they actually look like and whenever possible run a quick criminal and sex offender background check on them.

Very recently a lady I know told me she was dating, well really just chatting with a guy she met online and was in the security business. She asked me if I knew him, which I did not. She then sent me the link to his Facebook page which was very 'Gung Ho" but fell short on substance. It mostly showed the guy in macho poses, with guns and dressed in camo etc. She told me they were constantly messaging because he was working in Afghanistan with the US military and they would meet in person when he returned in a few months' time. She was excited as he was talking about his desire to get married and settle down etc. I saw some red flags but, she was happy and is a grown adult so should understand things.

Firstly, being former British Army myself I know what guys are like, especially when deployed, they are lonely and bored and that is just for starters. Also, talking about settling down with someone you have never met is not realistic, it might make for good conversation and creating a romantic mood but that's about it. Anyway, after a week or so I heard again from the lady. This time she told me she thought the guy was fake; I had to agree with her. She had previously sent me a photo of a trophy/challenge coin he claimed to have been awarded by the CIA for "Actions Under Fire", so now I sent her the eBay page where those coins were for sale for about $15. I did not tell her before as the guy may or may not have been full of shit, but she was happy.

She was surprised that a man would go to that extent to try to impress her and other women. I, on the other hand, am not at all surprised. She said he was always video chatting with her from a small military looking room, I told her it would not surprise me if he had built it in his mom's basement just for internet dating purposes... So, if you're meeting people online try to ensure you know who you are really talking to, the virtual world needs to be taken with a big grain of salt, nothing is real until proven.

One of the more conventional, organic ways of meeting people is in bars or nightclubs. Here at least you have a chance to see what they look like, how they smell etc. I believe all adults know the real reason men go to nightclubs is to pick up women. If you're still insisting you go for the atmosphere or the music you're lying to yourself. I think the term "Meat Market" best describes the bar and club scene and as long as people understand this then there are no problems.

I spent a lot of time in bars and clubs over the years, first when I was in the military and we practically lived in the clubs in Cyprus, and after that for many years as my company provided security for numerous venues, so I've seen a lot and I understand things. From a personal security point of view, there are a multitude of things that can go wrong in clubs ranging from theft, assaults and date rape.

I will talk about date rape later but even at a basic level be wary of people offering to buy you drinks, it's a classic guy tactic, get the girl drunk and she will have sex with you. Men also need to be careful of others buying them drinks as they could be set up for a sexual assault, gay rape does happen.

Quite a few times I have seen women trying to persuade one of their friends who is drunk not to go off with a guy or guys. The most recent was on South Beach in Miami where I was talking with some friends and we saw a girl who was clearly very drunk with 3 guys who, let's say did not look too respectable. Her friend was desperately trying to get her away from the guys but the girl who was drunk or maybe drugged did not appear to know what she wanted to do. Who knows what became of her, as they were walking quickly down Collins Avenue, and it was none of our business anyway. If her friend was that worried she should have called the police, but would the police respond? They would if they were told a girl was intoxicated and going to be sexually assaulted. However, if the police responded and the drunken girl said everything was ok no one could save her... And I am sure the cell phone videos of her sex party would quickly be spreading across the internet...

If you have children of a dating age you should start to inform them of the potential problems that can occur with dating. These days they need to be wise since just one bad experience can affect them for the rest of their lives.

Red flags

I tell people weather trying to build up business or personal relationships to always be on the lookout for potential red flags in a person's behavior or habits. Strangely, I think most people are a lot more cautious about their business dealings than they are about who they are dating, having sex with and letting into their family's life.

It takes time to know people and many times a relationship can start out fine and very quickly deteriorate. There is a huge difference between seeing someone a few nights a week to living with them, I have dated women I could tolerate for an evening but that's about it.

As you're getting to know someone look for red flags in their behavior for example, does what they tell you not match up with what you're seeing, have they lied about their backgrounds, are there drug or addiction issues, are they overly jealous and possessive or could they be cheating on you. Certain things will only come out over time, this is natural but red flags of extreme jealously or violence should be taken seriously as they could lead to domestic violence issues in the future.

Most people have secrets and have done things in the past they could be embarrassed about, ranging from being arrested, going to jail, addiction issues etc. Do people make mistakes and then change, yes... But if you're considering a serious relationship with someone and bringing them into your family, the good and bad about their and your past needs to be put on the table.

Gold diggers

I am sure many of you will say money does not come into consideration when you're looking to date someone; to that I will say bullshit, and this applies to men and women alike. I tell guys if they want to get laid all they need is a decent car and some cash to be able to take their dates out to nice locations, to spoil them, that's it. Most women will tolerate ugly guys with personality flaws if they are being spoiled and things are paid for.

I have known quite a few married men, with children who told me they know that if they lost their jobs and could not keep their wives in the same standard of living the wives would leave. I have come across some older and obnoxious men who are married to women half their age, and all I can say to those girls is: I hope you're getting enough financial benefits to do what you're doing. That's how the world works and if your relationship is built on financial dependence by either party then understand it can end when the money runs out or someone with a bigger wallet turns up.

A friend of mine whose sister deals with luxury real estate in South Florida, told me about one of the situations she encounters. Men are posing as interested buyers and arrive with their date to view million-dollar properties they have no intention or financial means to acquire, all for the sole purpose of impressing the lady.

Nowadays it's easy for a guy to prepare for a first date by renting a luxury vehicle and a nice room in an upscale hotel or Airbnb then taking his new lady friend to view luxury properties and Bingo! I would say in most cases the player is getting laid and he doesn't even care if he is found out after the fact as I am sure he has plenty of other young ladies lined up to give him a break from the mundane reality of his actual life.

So, be aware of being played by someone dating you just for money or ulterior motives. If you know it and you don't mind that's fine, it's your choice just remember to never get too emotionally attached.

One-night stands & sex

One-night stands can go bad in a lot of ways from major embarrassment to STD's. I can say you should never consider having one-night stands and casual sex but people do it all the time. All I am going to do here is make you aware of some of the risks.

I regularly encounter people who always carry hand sanitizer, eat only organic and would have a temper tantrum if the barista at their regular coffee shop used whole milk instead of non-fat soy milk in their morning latte, their bodies are temples after all! That being said, they have no problem taking illegal drugs and sleeping with virtual strangers; personally, I think this is a bit hypocritical.

Let me ask you this, think about the last person you kissed or gave you a polite peck on the cheek as a greeting, do you know where their mouth has been and what was in it during the last 24 hours? Have they been kissing or performing sexual acts on others? Now, the chances of them kissing or having sex with others multiplies if you pick them up in a club or hook up with them on holiday, be very aware of this. A lot of diseases can be spread orally so, you should really know what's been in the mouth of the person you're kissing, at least recently.

If you're having sex with relative strangers or are in an open relationship with someone you need to take hygiene very seriously. Even if you trust them you don't know what diseases their other sexual partners might have. Many people seem to have forgotten about HIV, but you know what, there is still no cure! In 2017 STD infection rates hit a record high in California with over 300,000 gonorrhea, chlamydia and syphilis alone, there are well over a million people with HIV in the US and in 2016 there were over 38,000 new cases. So, be very careful who you kiss!

Now if you go back to a stranger's hotel room or let them into your home you are posing a big risk to your personal security. To start with there is the risk of violence, the sex might turn out to be a lot rougher than you expected, they have friends waiting to join in or if you change your mind and want to go home they get angry and rape you anyway.

While in the Army I heard a story I can easily believe, about a young British soldier who was based in Germany and went to one of the local brothels and hired a hooker. She offered to make things a bit kinky and tie him up, which he agreed to. When he was well bound up, she let in the guys who had been waiting and they raped him. I'm sure such things happen a lot more that is known. Firstly, many guys don't want others to know they use prostitutes and secondly, they don't want others to know they were raped.

There have been many cases where people have been kidnapped or have disappeared after leaving a bar or club with someone they just met. Some turn up OK after a few days partying, many turn up dumped on a waste ground or in dumpsters. This is the risk you are taking every time you go home with a stranger.

Someone I knew was once worried about seeing a woman he had met online, an older and successful lady who could have also helped him with his career. The problem was the woman just wanted a sexual relationship and had made it known she sometimes liked to have sex with a couple of men at the same time. This made the guy I know nervous, he was OK with the casual relationship but was worried what would happen if during a group sex session, the other guy tried to have sex with him... My advice, don't get involved if you're uncomfortable with the situation, never be forced to have sex with others or perform sex acts you are not comfortable with. I have not heard from the guy in a long time and I am not sure if he took the woman up on her offer, maybe he did and had a life changing experience.

One of the big risks from a guy's perspective is that having sex with a woman creates the opportunity for her to cry rape or sexual assault and this generally means the guy is going straight to jail. This risk is multiplied if the girl is drunk or under the influence of drugs. You should always try to ensure you are dealing with mentally stable people because going home with the wrong person can literally ruin your whole life...

I don't judge people or their vices, if someone is into one-night stands or a swinger that's their choice but people need to understand their choices can also affect other people. A successful married businessman in his 50's met a girl at a strip club and offered to take her out on a date and she agreed. This man took the girl to dinner and the theater and when he took her home she asked him if he wanted to come up to her apartment to which of courses he said "Yes". What he did not know was the girl's boyfriend was waiting and watching.

After the couple were in the apartment for a short while the girl's boyfriend called the police and reported there was a woman screaming and being assaulted in the apartment. When the police turned up at the apartment the girl answered the door and confirmed the man would not leave and had tried to rape her. The once respectable businessman went straight to jail. To make things worse and to ensure he went to jail the girl had taken his ID's from his wallet.

So now the successful married businessman was sitting in jail on an attempted rape charge and needed to be bailed out. Some things are very difficult to hide from your spouse and this was one of them. The other issue arising from the attempted rape charge is, being a sex offence, if convicted he would be a registered sex offender and could kiss his business licenses goodbye. A few days after he was out of jail he received a phone call from the girl's boyfriend stating that for $30,000.00 she would drop the charge. That's when it became clear he had been set up from the beginning. I am not sure how things developed; he may have beaten the attempted rape charge, but he still had a lot of other personal problems to deal with.

You must remember that if you're taking strangers into your home you're also taking them into the lives of those you live with, if you have children I don't think it's wise, safe or mentally healthy for them to see a different lover popping in and out of your bedroom every weekend. If that is the lifestyle you like, then keep it separate from your family life and the lives of your children.

Taking them home

For those of you looking for a regular, long term relationship at some point, after you have checked out and are comfortable with your new partner, you will have to take them home or hang out at their place. There are multiple issues with taking people into your home especially if you have children.

On a basic security level, you don't want to bring someone into your house who could potentially steal from you or set you up to be burglarized. They could also bring or use drugs, which even if you are OK with, it's something children should not be exposed to. And let's not forget that if you get caught with drugs in your house you are legally responsible and most likely will be charged with possession. Another consideration when children are present is the compatibility between them and your new partner and how will they interact. It is imperative you assess the situation, consider all the potential issues and determine if your new partner will be a positive influence, before you open your home to them.

One problem I have heard of from multiple people, men and women, is that of the nightmare guest. You invite this person for a drink and either they start to make unwanted sexual advances and become aggressive when rebuffed or they flat out refuse to leave. I know of several ladies who had to call the police on such male friends. What I will say on this topic is make sure you establish clear boundaries and do not send mixed signals. Innocent flirting could be easily misconstrued as an invitation to have sex, especially when alcohol or drugs are involved.

Dating issues

Once in a relationship there are still plenty of potential security problems you need to be aware of. Remember it takes time to get to know someone and understand their past, so it's not really advisable to be doing such things as moving in together after only a few weeks. I have heard plenty of stories of couples moving in together only to realize after a short time they are not truly compatible which usually means the one who moved in needs to find somewhere else to live, and that is the "good case scenario". In the "bad case scenario" things get hostile and someone can end up homeless.

Another source of problems can be your partner's friends and family members. Someone might be a good person but the people they are surrounded with might be quite the opposite and the last type of people you want in your life. It's better to keep such people at arm's length rather than have to deal with others' drama and problems. If your partner has issues with this then maybe they are not the right one for you, as I have said before you need to be selective who you allow in your life especially if you have children.

Take the time to get to know people and don't rush into things, it's a fact that you're not going to know everything about someone even if you see and talk to them daily for a few months. Years ago a friend of mine had an issue with a lady he was in sort of a relationship with. This guy was working as a personal trainer when he met this woman who told him she was married, and her husband was OK with her having a boyfriend as he was gay and theirs was simply a cover marriage.

After a few months of seeing this lady my friend got a call from her husband who wanted to meet him... My friend agreed to meet him expecting the worse but as a former pro-fighter he knew he could handle the situation if trouble arose. When they met the husband listed all the hotels they had been to, restaurants they had been eating at etc. When my friend asked how he knew the husband told him it was because he was paying the bills for his wife's credit cards...

The husband went on to explain that yes, they had an open relationship, but he felt his wife was getting too serious and falling for my friend, he wanted her to be happy but not to divorce him for their children's sake. My friend told him he understood and that he would not see his wife again. The next time they saw each other he told her it was over without disclosing he spoke with her husband.

A few days later the lady's husband called my friend again and thanked him for ending the relationship with his wife. The husband was satisfied now that my friend was not just sleeping with her for her money and was not going to push her to get a divorce. He also stated he had told his wife about the meeting and she was upset that he had broken up their relationship, so he asked if my friend could start sleeping with her again... My friend refused as the situation was getting crazy; the husband called him a couple more times asking him to sleep with his wife but being old school, my friend just moved on. Hopefully you can better understand from this that you can never know how real someone's story is until you have known them for a long time.

I have heard several stories of women who have caught their partners cheating with other men. One of whom came home to find her husband having sex with another married man, the two men then attacked and beat the woman as they did not want her to tell anyone. When she got released from the hospital she moved out with her children and filed for a divorce, which was the right thing to do...

If you have children of dating age you need to know where they are and what they are doing, if they are borrowing your car to go on dates ensure they are not drinking and driving or taking drugs in the vehicle. You can get software to monitor their locations via their phones or just get a tracker in the car. Clearly explain to them the car is their responsibility and not to let their friends drive it or engage in any sort of illegal activity while in the vehicle etc...

Breaking up & stalkers....

If there are too many red flags or things are just not working out, then relationships should be ended. I don't see why people stay together if they are unhappy. Those who say they do it for the children's sake should consider the impact a stormy, dysfunctional relationship has on the children and realize everyone is much better off ending the relationship.

Now if you're dealing with a rational adult they will respect the fact a relationship is over and move on, sadly these days there is a major shortage of rational adults. I am sure we all have stories or know of stories of jealous or jilted ex's trying to get revenge on their former lovers. This is where things can get messy and dangerous so if things can be ended amicably try your best to do it. If there are red flags then cut all contact with your ex. Desperate people seek any attention and even if it's the negative kind it gives them hope of re-kindling things so, cut all communications, block them on social media, ignore all calls, messages and emails.

I know personally of one guy who stopped taking his diabetes medication when he was dumped and ended up in the hospital. The woman who dumped him was in total disbelief that he would go that far, jeopardizing his health and ultimately his life. When she went to the hospital to visit he even introduced her to his parents as his girlfriend... He wanted the attention and was trying to manipulate her into getting back together but she recognized the red flags and ended it.

If someone starts to stalk you then you need to take things seriously, start recording incidents, try to get a restraining order and increase your personal security, do not wait until it is too late.

DATE RAPE DRUGS

Think about how many times when you have been at bar or club or even a coffee shop and left your drink unattended, for less than 10 seconds with someone you have just met who seemed like a nice person. That would have been more than enough time for them to spike your drink with drugs such as Ketamine, GHB or Rohypnol. How often have you been in a bar or restaurant and the waiter or bartender has given you an open bottle of beer, soft drink or the like which could have been spiked with illegal drugs such as Ecstasy or prescription drugs such as Xanax? My guess is...many times!

I have spent more time than most in bars in developing countries and I can't remember being served a can of beer, bottle of beer or bottle of liquor that was not opened in front of me. The main reason is so the bars' patrons know they are getting what they ordered and not a cheaper brand of alcohol that has just been poured into a quality brand name bottle. This from a security perspective also makes it harder for the drinks to be spiked by the bar staff and waiters. I always tend avoid drinking draft beers or shots unless I can see the drinks being poured, to me that's not being paranoid it's being careful!

At this time, I am living in South Florida and regularly hear stories of males and females having their drinks spiked in bars and clubs. The motive is commonly thought of as "Date Rape" but this tactic is also used in robberies. There has been a change in rapist tactics where many have gone over to using prescription drugs which are widely available, especially in South Florida, as from a legal standpoint it's more difficult for the victims to argue they were drugged and not taking the drugs of their own accord. This is a common defense not only for the rapists and criminals but also the venues where people have initially been drugged, e.g., "we are not liable because you took the drugs when you were partying, no one spiked your drink!"

Gone are the days when people took responsibility for their actions, I would say that if it was reported to the management of most bars, clubs or casinos that a male or female had been drugged and raped in their venue the first thing their lawyers would be advising them is deny everything and wipe the CCTV footage. Why, because they don't want to be held liable for security negligence and they do not want the bad publicity. So, from the business standpoint it's better for them to deny any knowledge of the incident or make it seem the victim was intoxicated and what was going on appeared to be consensual. In areas where there is strict local authority or state licensing the venue will have problems but that's why they have attorneys. The victims, on the other hand, will have to rely on providing the police with sufficient witnesses and evidence of what really happened.

The next time you are out at a bar or restaurant take a look around and think about how easy it would be to drop a pill into someone's drink, this is the same thing rapists would be thinking. Now, if you're in a nightclub or party where there are dim lights, a lot of people and loud music the rapist, kidnapper or robber's job is a lot easier. If you really want to make it simple for the rapists etc. then let them go to the bar and buy you drinks... They are just being nice and you're getting free drinks, right...!

Rapists target males and females alike and in addition to the physical injuries of the assault there are also the issues of pregnancies and sexually transmitted diseases. Not only are drugs used for sexual assaults but also robberies. In South Florida it's common for men to meet a woman at a bar, have their drink spiked and be robbed of their Rolexes. If they manage to make it home before passing out they tend to lose a lot more. Some of these crimes are regularly reported and I expect a lot more are not.

Here is something for parents to think about: if you were out socializing and got drugged, the rapists or robbers find your ID's in your wallet and decide to take you back to your place to party, where your children are with maybe a teenage baby sitter... Not a very good and a potentially very messy situation from many angles... One bad choice can have a long term negative effect on the lives of all of your family!

Many sexual assaults where the victims have been drugged are not reported to police for many reasons ranging from the victims not wanting the social stigma rape carries to the uncertainty of who rapped them. If someone is rapped they must see a doctor due to the risk of pregnancy and sexually transmitted diseases. They should report the crime because if this person has raped once, they most probably have done it before and will do it again, they are a sexual predator and need to be behind bars. Police departments have specially trained officers to deal with sexual assault and rape cases and they need to be informed as soon as possible after an assault because they need to start gathering evidence. If you have a friend who has been raped or sexually assaulted and they do not want to talk to the police, do what you can to change their minds, this is for everyone's sake, no just theirs.

You don't have to go to bars and nightclubs to be exposed to the risk of being drugged, one Gypsy tactic in Europe is to get their small children to go out and sell glasses of tea or soft drinks to tourists. Who would expect a little girl to give you a spiked drink? The children are accompanied by teenagers who then watch and follow the victims until they pass out or go and help them when they start to stumble, at which time they rob, rape or kidnap them.

A drug that is regularly used in crimes in Colombia, Venezuela and Ecuador is Burandanga or Scopolamine which is extracted from the Borrachero tree. Scopolamine has numerous legitimate medical uses but when used by rapists and criminals it renders their victims into a compliant zombie- like state of which they remember nothing. Victims have the outward appearance of being okay but are in fact in a trance and know nothing of what they're doing. Victims of Scopolamine overdoses are common in Colombian hospitals as are the deaths of those who received a large dose or had a low tolerance. This drug is more common than people think and is out there. I have come across similar incidents in Haiti and West Africa where the drug, once administered in liquid or powder form makes the victim completely compliant and helpless.

The common date rape drugs like Rohypnol, GHB, Ketamine are tasteless and odorless and take approximately 15 to 30 minutes to take effect and usually last three to six hours, depending on dosage. These drugs make the victims weak, making them unconscious and unable to remember what happened. Prescription drugs such as Klonopin and Xanax have similar effects, all of which are enhanced when the victim had been drinking alcohol.

In many places, such as non-first-world countries, especially those popular with tourists the police will try to dismiss cases of sexual assault and rape because they don't want to work or want to avoid the bad publicity for their resorts etc. The fact you were drugged will be blamed on the fact you were partying, you got drunk, took the drugs yourself and agreed to have sex, prove different! In some Middle Eastern countries if a rape is reported, especially by a female, the victim can end up in jail and charged for sex out of marriage, after serving a term in prison they will be deported, if the rapist was a local the chances are the police investigation would be minimal if any, while the victims have to deal with the trauma of the attack, possible sexually transmitted diseases and pregnancies...

If you are out at a bar, club or just accepted a drink from a stranger and start to feel weak or dizzy for no apparent reason get help immediately. Get to a safe location, get to trusted friends, call your friends or family, even call an ambulance but do not go with strangers. Hopefully you can see it's better to be careful and perceived as paranoid than it is to end up drugged, abused and dumped in the gutter!

DRUGS

Dealing with drug and substance abuse is another subject that could fill multiple books and to be honest I am not an expert in the matter, in this chapter I will be high-lighting some of the problems I have encountered over the years and how parents can help protect their children.

I will mainly talk about mainstream drugs in this chapter, but you must also remember substances such as solvents are still used by many to get high and are very addictive. Drugs these days are widely available legally and illegally and for many teens can be easier to buy and use than alcohol. Teens can buy or be given illegal drugs, steal prescription drugs from their parents or actually have been prescribed them by irresponsible doctors.

Street drugs

People make me laugh when they are fussy eaters, especially those who go on about how their body is a temple and only eat organic foods or the won't eat meat etc. but they will buy drugs from a street dealer and put them in their body without knowing where they came from or what it is they are really taking.

At basic street business level, the drug dealer wants to make money, that's why they are selling drugs. They want to get you addicted, because you will buy more drugs, it's business and you are the commodity. There only worries about you is that if you're arrested or overdose that you will inform on them to the police and you might not be buying drugs from them while you're in jail or hospital.

Drug dealers don't only frequent housing projects and council estates as portrayed in the movies, they operate everywhere there are potential clients. The best markets for them are where people have plenty of money and want to party so, not only night clubs are a choice location but also schools and universities, especially those where the kids' parents give them decent allowances.

Again, as a parent you need to educate your children to the risks of getting involved in the drug world weather they are using or have the stupid idea to start selling to make some easy money. The drug world is a criminal world even though now in many places Marijuana is being legalized it is still a very shady business.

Violence is part of the drug world and can kick off due to debts, people being ripped off on deals or over territory disputes.

Now think about it at base level, if someone goes to buy drugs from a street dealer, what's stopping the dealer from just robbing them, what are they going to do, call the police and say the guy they went to buy drugs from robbed them? What are they going to do if the dealer gives them something which is not drugs, call the police to complain?

I know of one guy in London who, after a night drinking, bought what he thought was Hash from some guys on the street in Brixton but, when he tried to smoke it he realized they had sold him an OXO cube (beef stock cube used for cooking) and was not happy. He went back and confronted the OXO cube dealers and lucky for them he was too drunk to be able to hit them with his motorcycle helmet, he tried but missed... When Brixton Police saw the commotion and intervened, he told them the whole story which brought smiles to everyone's face. Luckily this guy's brother was with him so the cop's advice was go home before being arrested for being drunk and disorderly and, don't try to ride your bike or you will be arrested for drunk driving... Luckily his brother managed to get him into a taxi. This is a funny story but BS like this happens all the time and can get people hurt and into a lot of trouble on all sides.

To buy drugs you must deal with shady people. How do you know what you're buying? Is it what you want, is it good for you, is it poison? Do you think those manufacturing the pills and cocaine care if you die? How many people have been killed in the drugs wars and how many killed just to get those drugs in your hands? So, if you're poisoned or overdose who cares? Possibly your family and the dealer will if you owe money but that's about it.

I mentioned in the chapter on sexual predators about a girl who was possibly sold to traffickers to pay off other drugs debts; this does happen. Drug addicts do whatever they have to do to get the drugs they crave, be it sexual favors, stealing, prostitution or even selling or prostituting their children.

I am sure many who have used illegal recreational drugs and are reading this will be thinking they would never become an addict. Well, if the drugs you are taking are laced with substances you didn't know about it might not be your choice. If you are a parent ensure your children know not to take pills or smoke drugs, especially if they are offered by a stranger or older person. This is a classic sexual predator's tactic with the aim of getting the child addicted and depended on them as their supplier, they can then abuse or prostitute the child as they wish.

Prescription drugs

At the time of writing this the U.S. is undergoing a major opioid abuse epidemic. In 2016 alone there were over 63,000 deaths due to drug over doses and over 60% of those were due to opioids. In 2016 11.5 million Americans from the age of 12 years and up misused prescribed medications. 80% of the opioids produced globally are sold and used in the United States.

So, what are opioids? Opioids are pain killers made to replicate the effects of opium. Prescription opioids include morphine, oxycodone, or hydrocodone, illegal opioids include heroin and fentanyl. Opioids should only be used for a limited period of time for cases of extreme pain, but in the US it's reported that 99% of doctors issue prescriptions over the 3-day recommended limit for the drugs. Opioids give the users a feeling of calm, relaxation in addition to numbing pain, the same as opium.

If it is known that opioids are so dangerous and addictive then why do doctors in the US over prescribe them so much, well the answer is simple, MONEY! What a lot of people outside of the US may not understand is that the health care and medical system in the US is a private business and services need to be paid for, usually by the patient's insurance. A lot of US doctors are just legal drug dealers, they have a license, street dealers don't!

I am sure a lot of what I am going to say here will piss off a lot people, but I am going to say: suck it as you need to fucking hear it!!! I was always under the impression that people became doctors because they wanted to help people and it was a very respectable profession. Today, in the US at least, I believe those entering the medical profession are doing so to make a lot of money and all the sick people are just the commodity to make the money off.

Now, I'm sure some of you are saying that I would not be writing this if I needed a doctor's help. Ok, the word is not "help" it's "services", help is generally free, services you pay for. If I go to the hospital or doctor's office I pay for their time and services, no different than taking my car to a mechanic, and the standard of service I receive depends on how much I pay. I know people who have taken their cars to bad mechanics and the cars have broken down shortly after apparently being fixed, I also know several people who had bad doctors and died due minor complications and mishaps...

I have also known very well several people who had severe issues, one of them fatal, because they became addicted to prescription medications. Here is an example of how easy it is for someone to get such things as prescription anti-depressants in Florida, US. My ex-wife after our fairly amicable divorce went to her doctor for a checkup, when she let it slip that she was recently divorced the doctor gave her a free sample of anti-depressants. She was not there because she was feeling depressed, she never complained to the doctor about being depressed, to be honest I think we were both in a state of relief and had not been so happy in years. So, why did the doctor give her the pills? I am sure he was hoping she would take them and like the feeling they gave her, and then she would buy some more, regularly... She flushed them and did not go back to that doctor again.

I am sure some readying this are thinking what I meant by free sample. Physicians in the US are provided with free samples of drugs by the sales reps for the drug companies. If doctors prescribe drugs, from what I understand, they make a percentage from each sale, so it's in the doctor's financial interests to write prescriptions. As one doctor I once knew in the US used to say all the time "a patient cured is a client lost". Sadly, this is the mentality of the pharmaceutical companies, their sales reps and the majority of US doctors.

I avoid going to doctors in the US because I don't trust them, their interests are in making money not my health. I am very anti-drug anyway and would sooner trust a traditional Chinese doctor any day... From what you have read so far you should be able to see that US doctors are looking for reasons to medicate their patient's and diagnose them with some disease.

I know of one lady whose daughter had been getting into trouble and took her to her doctor, then to a phycologist who diagnosed the girl as being bipolar, which left the mother in shock. Wisely she went to another phycologist for a second opinion who told her the daughter was not bipolar, just going through a rebellious stage and would grow out of it, which she did,

Why, in a medical professional right mind would they want to diagnose a child with a mental disorder that they did not have, which could affect them for the rest of their lives? Do you know how many pills someone who is bipolar needs to take to control their condition? A lot! Their conditions need to be monitored, medications adjusted etc, etc... So, a young bipolar patient is a nice source of income for the unscrupulous medical professional...

I think I can honestly say I have been in more "shit hole" countries than most people and dealt with many in those countries who live in poverty, have experienced things people in developed countries cannot comprehend. But I don't think I have ever came across anyone claiming to suffer from depression or anxiety, I don't think they have time for such things as they have lives to get on with and usually families to feed. Maybe the fact they are used to living in harsh condition and have responsibilities to take care of means such feelings of depression and anxiety are things they comprehend or if they do experience them they have the mental strength to keep on living as normal.

Not quite the same in the US, a place where I come across so many people claiming to be suffering from and taking medications for depression or anxiety. The US is a very safe country with a very high standard of living, so why is everyone anxious and depressed? Because their car is over two years old, they can't afford a new 65-inch TV this year, someone wrote a nasty comment on one of their Facebook posts? Get a grip people, I think a good slap on the back of the head or kick in the ass would work a lot better than the pills you're popping!

Another reason they could have been suffering from depression or anxiety is because the doctor who prescribed them their "happy pills" told them they were. This has been a big problem with Military Veterans who have reported to their doctors that they have issues sleeping etc. Instead of recommending healthy diets and exercise the doctors diagnose depression, anxiety or PTSD and start writing prescriptions.

Human beings have been going through traumatic events and rough times since they evolved well over a million years ago but in the last 20 years, millions of people have started to need pills to deal with life's minor ups and downs, which is crazy.

One American guy I know who married a European girl whose family lived in the US told me that when he first met her family, one of them said to him after an hour or so that he did not act like most Americans they knew. When he asked them why they laughed and said they had been chatting for over an hour and he had not mentioned anything about what illnesses he had or what medications he was taking. I understand their point, it seems to have become the norm for everyone to be sick in some way and be taking medications for something, which is pretty disturbing.

From what I see it has become trendy to claim to suffer from such things as depression or anxiety. I have had people working for me claim they had recently been suffering from depression and anxiety, that's why they screwed up jobs; more like they were lazy and incompetent. I am old school and understand times are changing, when I was a kid John Wayne and Clint Eastwood were boy's role models today it's things like Justin Bieber.

I understand the doctors and the pharmaceutical companies' motivation for wrongly diagnosing and over medicating the US population, but I don't understand why people tolerate it. It's been claimed by many and I believe it 100% that all of the mass and school shooters in recent US history have been on some type of prescription drugs for a mental illness such as anxiety, depression or behavioral issues, such little facts tend to be kept out of the media. Should they have been able to buy guns if being diagnose with mental issues, NO! But, did they have mental issues or were just being prescribed concoctions of mind altering pills for illnesses they never had.

The pharmaceutical companies are making billions of dollars form the drug market in the US and can afford to employ the top lobbyists in Washington D.C.. I am also sure they give plenty of donations to political campaigns across the US to ensure the status quo. Which has been failing in the states that have legalized medical and recreational marijuana. I think these states have realized they can make a lot more money taxing marijuana than they do from the pharmaceutical companies, again we are back to money.

A story to finish this section came from a very good friend of mine who was working in the legal marijuana business in California. A lady who was a close relative of one of his friend was diagnosed with cancer and was told it was terminal, so she returned to her country to die. Of course, her family members were extremely upset about this and arranged for her a supply of cannabis oil as a last-ditch attempt to save her, it worked, and she recovered. When she returned to the US she went to see her doctor he was surprised to see her... He then started lecturing her that what she had done was illegal etc. etc... Think he was upset he did not get his commission...

The benefits of cannabis oil and marijuana have been known for a long time, but there is too much money involved in cancer treatments etc. for the pharmaceutical companies to want it legalized, hopefully things are changing.

As I said earlier, I don't trust US doctors, I am very sure there are some very good ones but to trust just one person's opinion on your or your child's health is very irresponsible. For anything remotely serious seek multiple opinions before committing to any medication programs etc. Remember to the medical industry, you and your loved ones are the commodity and they want you sick!

Over the years I have had several encounters with guys who I would say were over using steroids for bodybuilding and strength training. From what I understand to use steroids, testosterone or growth hormones safely, if there is a safe way, you have to know what you are doing, or you can seriously damage your health.

In the last section on prescription drugs I focused on the issues in the US but another area with similar developing prescription drug issues is the Arab Gulf States. Also, in a lot of Middle Eastern countries such things as steroids are not highly regulated, if at all. Bodybuilding is big in many places and guys and girls wanting to put on muscle fast tend to turn to the Steroids for help!

In addition to gaining muscle the side effects of steroid use in men can include developing breasts, becoming impotent and infertile. Side effects in women include excessive face and body hair and having their voices deepen. Indicators that people are on steroids can include acne, mood swings, flying into rages, suffering delusions, going bald and yellowing of skin. The long-term health risks include an enlarged heart, a high-risk of heart attacks, liver disease and liver cancer. All of these health risks are multiplied if the users don't know how to properly use the steroids or are not using quality products.

I will give you some quick stories on steroids use, the first is from when I was working as a freelance bouncer etc. in London. At one of the venues there was guy who initially was cool but over the course of say 12 months no one wanted to work with due to his let's say, unstable behavior. Over that 12-month period he had put on muscle and developed quite bad acne, so most people knew what his issues was were.

One night he was working with another guy who was known to be a bit hot tempered, they ended up having to throw someone out of the venue which was not uncommon as the place could get a little bit rough at times. The problem was that when ejecting the guy who was being pain they did so by opening the fire escape door with his head, which left a nice gash... To top it off when to police checked the CCTV they had some nice video of the guys giving the drunk a good kicking while he was on the ground.

At the time, the guy who was on steroids was a student in his early 20's and because he wanted to put on muscle quickly ended up with a lot of problems. From what I remember his family hired a good attorney for him and he ended up with a suspended sentence and the reason he got that and did not go to jail is because his attorney argued he was out of control due to excessive steroid use, which he was.

Another example comes from two guys who attended one of my close protection courses in South Florida, both big guys, ex-military, one was ex-police also. What I noticed was they were drinking a lot of water and they needed multiple breaks to eat.

On my close protection courses we work long hours and food breaks are not a priority, and these guys would get very agitated if we worked for too long; clearly something was not right, anyway they lasted for two days of a four-day course, they had paid so, thank you.

On one of the following courses I had a student who was a personal trainer and into natural bodybuilding and he asked me about one of the business cards in my office, which had belonged to one of the two previous students. I don't think I had read the cards, but the student pointed out the card was advertising what could be interpreted in the bodybuilding world for steroids; it was then their behavior made sense.

If you're working out and someone suggests that you start using steroids be very careful. If you have a child who is an athlete, make sure they know the problems that can come with steroid use and monitor their behavior!

Signs of addiction & drug use

I have not spoken about the different categories of drugs or the many different types in this chapter as I think that it's pretty irrelevant, a drug is a drug. As a parent you want to ensure your child steers clear of all addictive substances, whatever that are. Below are a few indicators that someone may be using drugs, if someone has multiple of these indicators then you need to take action before things get out of control.

- Stars to be absent from work or school on a regular basis.
- They miss work or school project deadlines.
- Their work ethic become slow and sloppy.
- They seem to be having multiple accidents and making simple mistakes regularly.
- They are constantly complaining and showing signs of depression.
- Things start to go missing from your home or their friends complain of things disappearing.
- They lose interest in work, their old friends and social activities.
- Explosive arguments and emotional outbursts occur over minor issues.
- They seem to be in a constant hangover.
- They start to use drug culture slang and avoid non-users.
- They start to become secretive.

- They lose interest in their appearance and hygiene.
- They become erratic, forgetful, indecisive and easily excitable.
- They display nervous behavior such as the drumming of fingers or foot tapping.
- They are constantly restless and hyper-excitable.
- They are constantly tired and fatigued.
- Their co-ordination lapses, they become very awkward.
- They have a constant runny nose, coughs or sore throats.
- Their eyes have large (dilated) or small pupils, are bloodshot or watery.
- They start to slur their speech and change their speech pattern.
- They constantly pick and scratch their arms etc.
- They have blood spots and small bruises on the arms and legs.
- They start to wear long sleeve clothes even in hot weather.
- They have a sweet acrid smell about them.
- They always need money.
- They have in their possession drug paraphernalia such as hypodermic needles, aluminum foil, mirrors, straws, glass pipes, capsules, vials, cigarette lighters or small butane torches etc.
- They admit to having or you find drugs in their possession.

If you believe someone is experimenting with drugs or becoming addicted, you must educate them to the potential problems and get them professional help. These days drug use has been glamorized by Hollywood and main stream entertainers, but the reality is far from glamourous. Dealers tend to go to jail, if they don't get killed and addicts end up on the street committing BS crimes or prostitution trying to get the money for their next fix. As for the recreational users, you're walking a very fine line and I hope you stay lucky, I also hope you won't pass your bad habits on to your children, who might not be as lucky as you!

Domestic violence and abuse is a very complicated issue for those directly involved and can be even more complicated for those trying to help the victims. When we talk about domestic violence everyone tends to think of a husband beating up his wife, but it is a lot more complicated than that and can take many forms. How people get into abusive relationships and why they stay in them is a whole other book that I am not qualified to write, so in this chapter I will give you my opinions and some examples of issues I have encountered.

Personally, I see no reason being in a relationship, however casual or serious if the other person annoys you, belittles you or is abusive, life is too short to deal with assholes. But, I regularly come across people who are in unhappy relationships and their reasons for staying in the relationship are for their children's sake, for financial reasons or because the sex is good etc. I can understand it to an extent but if you're unhappy then should you not be trying to find a better option, become independent and find a better partner, if you must have one.

The only reason why I can understand someone temporarily staying in an abusive relationship is to protect their children until they can be financially independent enough to take them and leave. Staying in an abusive relationship is only going to lead to more problems whether it's violence or issues with the law, and many times it's the innocent party that ends up getting arrested.

I have heard of plenty of cases where the husband or boyfriend were the ones suffering the physical abuse, a little bit of a change on the stereotype right! The problems for guys in this situation are very complicated... Most men are still brought up not to hit a woman, even in self-defense and I am sure most of you reading this will agree. Well, from my experience I have come across many women that are far more aggressive than most men and could drop most men easily. One of the issues with men defending themselves against a woman's attack is the law tends to always side with the woman, this is fact. So, guys, your best option if you're dealing with a violent woman is to end the relationship and avoid her, do not give her the opportunity to create a problem for you that could land you in jail.

The other problem for guys is the social stigma that goes with others knowing that they are being beaten by their wives or girlfriends. These days I think people understand that women can be abusive to their partners and that you're doing the right thing to end a relationship based on that reason. It's not emasculating, the opposite, you tolerated it, you did not retaliate, ended it and moved on, the right thing to do.

Everyone needs to understand that many people thrive on negative attention and love having drama in their lives for multiple reasons. Personally, I avoid such people like the plague and the main reason I deal with a very small and selective circle of people these days, most of which I still keep at arm's length. I have come across people that have gone out of their way to cause problems for their partners for no rational reasons, if there was a reason then it was minor. I think in many cases drugs were involved and these people just liked being in a state of constant crisis. Such people need to be avoided, they can be fun for a casual relationship but end it amicably before things go bad.

Being the innocent party and getting arrested is a very common thing to happen in domestic violence cases. In the US most police departments have a policy that if they are called to a domestic incident someone has to go to jail, this is mainly for liability reasons as they don't want to be sued if someone was hurt after they left. No evidence of violence is necessary, the simple fact a couple is having a loud argument can land someone in jail, so be warned.

One lady I know was in a relationship with a guy who had a binge drinking issue. She was at his home, in a rural part of the US, and one evening he started drinking and arguing so she decided to leave. As he had driven her there she had to call a taxi and in the meantime, he called the police to tell them he wanted her out of his home. The police arrived before the taxi and even though he was the one intoxicated they arrested the lady, as someone had to go to jail. She said the cops were extremely nice and apologetic, but rules are rules.

When the boyfriend realized what had happened he drove drunk to the police station to ask them to release her, it was a mistake, whereupon he was arrested for drunk driving. The lady was quickly released and not charged but she now has an arrest on her record for domestic violence... She is a very educated professional from a very conservative background and this was an extremely traumatic event for her. Can this be classed as domestic abuse, I would say yes, getting people arrested for no reason is not a joke.

Several years ago, I was doing business in Haiti and had just returned from a trip there with my Haitian/American business associate. As he was going through his mail in our office he showed me a letter from the State of Florida telling him to hand in his firearms as he had been accused of domestic violence, so he could not be in possession of firearms or ammunition until the case was resolved. He did not know what the accusation was for and if he had arrest warrants out for him he wanted to find out as he wanted things clarified and resolved ASAP. So, we both went to the Miami Dade Police Headquarters where he presented the letter and explained to the officer at the desk that he did not know what the accusations were about, but if he had warrants he was there to turn himself in. The desk officer checked and my associated had no warrants, the officer then explained that in Florida domestic violence complaints can be filed in Civil Family Court without need for police involvement or evidence.

To make a long story short the complaints against him were from an ex-girlfriend and her main complaint was he had been using Voodoo against her, including on dates when we were in Haiti. For a white man I think I understand more than most about African, Haitian and Latin magic, as crazy as that might sound to some of you. My associate had been complaining eggs had been broken on his car and the front door of his home, eggs are used in a lot of magic rituals. He had also mentioned that items had been put out side of his home that could be related to voodoo rituals and his wife was not happy...

The case went to court and there were two hearings, the judge was an older Cuban lady who I am sure understood how voodoo and santería were viewed and used in the Haitian and Latin communities. So, in addition to his attorney fees my associate ended up with a six-month restraining order against him. Only in Miami, right....!

Now obviously my Haitian associate's issues stemmed from a very jealous ex-girlfriend, note jealousy can be extremely dangerous and lead people to act completely irrationally. A good example of this is that of a respected professional man who had legal custody of his two children and was put through a crazy ordeal by his ex-wife and her mother who were not even in the same country with him.

This gentleman who lives in a very nice area in the US was woken by police hammering on his door late one night; when he answered the door the officers told him to keep his hands where they could see them and demanded to see his daughters. They had received a complaint that he had hit and choked one of them... The police had turned up prepared to deal with a child abuse situation and had the paramedics and social services with them.

The source of the complaint against the gentleman was his ex-mother in law who was living in Venezuela. One of the daughters had complained to the grandmother that her father had sent her to bed early, the grandmother then called the police in the US from Venezuela and told them her granddaughter was being beaten. When the police and social services spoke with his daughters and saw there was no issues they left and explained they were just doing their job, which the gentleman respected. He had problems with his ex-wife in the past and his attorney was made aware the police had turned up on his door as soon as he was allowed to make a phone call.

The next morning, he was making breakfast for his daughters when there was a hammering on his front door; when he opened the door the police officers who were there handcuffed him at gun point and then entered his house with social services to check on his daughter as they had received a call that they were being abused... Which they were not, they were waiting for their breakfast... This time his ex-wife had called the police from Panama, where she was on vacation with her new boyfriend to report her daughters were being abused... Again, after the police and social services spoke with his daughters and saw there were no issues they left and explained they were just doing their job.

Can this be classed as domestic abuse, in my books yes, this man's ex-wife was using the police to harass him. How do you think this affected the children, to be woken up late at night to be interviewed by the police, to see their father handcuffed at gunpoint in the morning etc. In addition to the drama and the upset caused to his children this guy had more attorney fees to deal with. The good thing from this episode is that the irrational and irresponsible behavior of his ex-wife helps ensure that he will keep the custody of his children.

If you are dealing with a jealous and vengeful ex-partner be aware of the risk of them calling the police on you for some fictitious reasons or using the legal system to cause you problems. Remember, if the police turn up on your door step they are just responding to a call, they have no idea of the real situation, always remain calm however upset you are. Getting into a fight with the police will not help you, if the issue has to do with child custody any altercations you have with the police will work against you, and most jealous ex's will know this. All you can do is be aware of your legal rights, get a good attorney and don't do anything stupid.

Dealing with violence

If someone is dealing with a violent partner they should leave the relationship immediately. Again, I understand some people will tolerate it, hoping things get better etc. That's their choice, if people don't want to listen then it's up to them to deal with the consequences, which can be difficult to accept for those close to them trying to help but it's their choice. If children are involved in the situation things become very complicated and concerned family members or friends need to get some professional legal advice on what they can do to help. Laws vary greatly from location to location so do your research. If it's obvious the children are being beaten or abused the police need to be informed immediately.

When dealing with violence you need to know your rights and the laws on self-defense, which vary greatly from area to area. I have heard of many situations where women would have been 100% justified to shoot their abusers but had no clue what to do in a violent situation. If you know your partner can become violent have some plans in place of what to do if they turn on you or your children. The best option is always to leave and go somewhere safe, if you can't then you need to consider your options for self-defense. I have heard ladies say they would feel guilty hurting their violent husband or getting him sent to jail... All I can say is it would be nice if he felt the same when he was beating them...

To finish this chapter, I will present an example from a lady I knew who went from being on her final stretch to become an accomplished academic to virtually ending up on the streets homeless. This lady got into a relationship with a guy who would be the last person you expect to be a wife beater, judging by his public persona... He was a cartoonist and his works have been featured in some high-profile media campaigns etc...

The lady should have picked up on the red flags when he insisted she sell her defensive firearms on grounds he was anti-guns, started to isolate her from her friends and spending her money. He was taking control of her... After their marriage, when he received his US residency and her money started to run out the issues began, many of which I am sure I'm not aware of and I am not interested in. What I do know is that she started taking prescription drugs, started self-harming, attempted suicide a few times and ended up Baker acted, I believe on several occasions. The turnaround point was when she finally got the strength to call the police on him, get him arrested and then get a divorce. I understand a few days in Rikers Island gave him a reality check... She was then able to try to start to recover and put her life back together.... Best not to get into such situations in the first place, right....!

CHILD ABUSE

I have spoken about child abuse in various parts of this book and mainly focused on sexual abuse and predators. In this chapter we will talk more about the effects of child abuse and also child neglect.

It's a very sad fact that children are usually abused by those that know them and their family or are in positions of trust. The implication of child abuse and neglect can have lifelong implications for the victims. Children who experience abuse and neglect have a high-risk of behavioral, emotional and mental issues as an adult.

Victims of child abuse and neglect are at a high-risk from complications in their adult lives such as depression, anxiety, poor self-esteem, aggressive behavior, eating disorders, drug/alcohol abuse, self-abuse and suicide attempts. I spoke with Trent Steel, the President of the Anti-Predator Project in Miami and a Counselor and asked his about the effects child abuse and neglect can have on the victims in later life.

Trent stated: "The realm of Child Abuse is a very broad subject and can take many forms from physical, sexual, emotional and psychological. The effects on the child during childhood and in later life can be very damaging and destructive to them and those around them."

To generalize in the early years a child who is a victim of abuse can seem to be withdrawn and quiet or subject to aggressive and violent outbursts. In their teenage years the victim can become rebellious, sexually promiscuous and start to experiment with alcohol and drugs, all of which will affect their education and put them at a very high-risk of getting in trouble with the police. In adult life the victim can have problems with severe drug/alcohol abuse, criminal behavior, keeping a job, developing and maintaining relationships.

Some victims, especially those who are being subjected to sexual abuse tend to hide the abuse they are suffering from others, especially their families. For the caring family the apparently groundless disruptive behavior of the child can lead them to discipline the child, without seeking to find the cause of the child's issues, which further alienates the child. Don't get me wrong, children can be disruptive without any abuse being present and need to be disciplined but, parents and caregivers should always be alert for signs of abuse.

In extreme cases self-harm such as the victim cutting or burning themselves can be present as is the risk of suicide. In the US suicide is the second main cause for deaths in young people aged from 15 to 24. There have been many cases where emotional abuse such as bullying at school or online bullying has lead a child to commit suicide. A lot of children these days do not have the resilience that children of previous generations had and are greatly affected by name calling or embarrassing or inappropriate photos of them being posted online etc. Parents and caregivers must monitor the child and identify the sources of abuse or distress to a child before the situation gets out of hand for all involved.

The types of child abuse

Child abuse can take many forms ranging from excessive disciplining to trafficking for child labor or sexual exploitation. In many cases those committing or enabling the abuse are known to the child and can be classed as apparently trusted family members or caregivers. Remember, if you are responsible for a child, even for a short period of time, and if the child comes to harm you will be held responsible.

- **Physical abuse:** In very young children rough handling and shaking can easily lead to broken bones, concussions and possible deaths. Excessive disciplining such as beating, kicking or whipping a child can lead to sever injuries, both physically and psychologically. Withholding medical treatment for a sick or injured child is also classed as a form of abuse. Anything that intentionally damages a child's wellbeing is abuse.
- **Sexual abuse:** Rape is not the only form of sexual abuse, someone inappropriately touching a child or have a child inappropriately touch them is abuse.
- **Emotional abuse:** This form of abuse is the most difficult to detect and is often overlooked as it leaves no physical marks but can be just as, if not more destructive to a child than regular beatings. Continuous threats, intimidation, belittling and bullying can lead to long-term mental health issues. Those who have suffered from emotional abuse run a high-risks of developing depression, anxiety, low self-esteem, relationship problems, alcohol/drug problems and suicidal tendencies.
- **Neglect:** Child neglect is where a parent or care giver neglects their duty to care for and provide a child a safe environment. Leaving a child unattended in a room where it can harm itself is neglect as is leaving a child unattended in a

car, even for a short period of time. If a child is kept in unsanitary conditions, not kept clean or properly fed, it is neglect and those responsible for the child can be arrested and charged.

Recognizing the signs of abuse and neglect

It is important for parents and care givers to be able recognize high-risk situations and the signs of abuse and neglect in children. If you suspect a child is being abused or neglected reporting your suspicions can help protect the child and can help get the family the necessary support and assistance they possibly need. The following are possible signs of child abuse or neglect.

- The child shows sudden changes in their behavior such as being withdrawn, mood swings or temper tantrums.
- The child shows extreme behavior, such as being overly compliant or demanding, extremely passive or aggressive.
- The child has physical or medical problems that are not being attended to by the parents or caregiver
- The child has abnormal learning problems or difficulty concentrating
- The child is watchful, always nervous, anxious and defensive as if expecting something bad to happen
- The child is constantly dirty and smells from not being washed
- The child uses alcohol or drugs
- The child does not have proper adult supervision, states there is no-one at home to take care of them
- The child is inappropriately infantile, such as frequently rocking or head-banging etc.
- The child states a lack of attachment or dislike for their parents or care giver
- The child runs away from home, self-harms or attempts suicide
- The child's parent or care giver shows little interest in the child or openly rejects it
- The child's parent or care giver seems to be depressed of suffering from emotional distress
- The child's parent or care giver is abusing drugs or alcohol
- The child's parent or care giver shows signs or irrational behavior or acts aggressively towards the child
- The child's parent or care giver constantly criticizes, belittles and humiliates the child

Hope fully this chapter has highlighted the very complicated and common problem of child abuse. As responsible parents you must be aware of the problem and educate others on the signs and what to do if child abuse or neglect is suspected.

DOMESTIC KIDNAPPING
& CHILD RECOVERY

The domestic kidnapping of children is a common issue in messy divorces or why a single parent has custody of the child. I know of cases when single mothers have never told the biological fathers that the children were born because they did not want issues with the custody of the child or the fathers in the child's life. I can understand this and to be honest their choices are none of my business. The women all said they were worried about the fathers finding out and then trying to get custody of the child, especially when the mothers had a lot more money and assets than the fathers.

This chapter I wrote as an article for security professionals and those involved in the world of kidnap and ransom, but it will give everybody a glimpse into an issue that can affect all parents.

Domestic child kidnapping

Domestic child kidnapping & child recovery is an area of the security and investigation industry that is much talked about and glamorized but in reality, can be classed as criminal activity.

There are many cases where an estranged parent will take a child they do not have legal custody for and flee to a foreign country. These days international travel is not complicated as long as you have a valid passport and visas, if required. If the estranged parent has a passport or papers for the child to travel all they have to do is cross a border and any legal custody judgments for the child are usually void as the local country's laws usually take precedence. The Hague Child Abduction Convention is the international law that tends to be used for child custody disputes but how this is interpreted at local levels is another thing.

A single parent may have custody of their child in U.S. etc. but if their ex-partner is a citizen of say an European country and manages to kidnap and take the child to their own country and then applies for custody of the child there, the local courts will most probably rule in their favor, after lengthy court proceedings. I have been asked quite a few times if I could go to various countries to recover children who have been taken by estranged parents. I am happy to provide advice and highlight the fact that if the parent I am talking too has legal custody in U.S. this might not apply in the country the child is in.

I know of one gentleman who had full legal custody of his child in the U.S. but his ex-wife, during an un-supervised visitation with the child, managed to get them on a plane and back the Western European country where she was from and lived. This gentleman who had full custody of the child in the US went to Europe, located the child and snatched the child in the street from one of his ex-wife's family members. The local police arrested him before he made it to the airport and luckily for him they were very understanding. They explained that his ex-wife had started legal proceedings for the child in that country and what he had done could be classed as attempted kidnapping, but they understood his situation. They released him with the advice that if he tried it again he would be charged with attempted kidnapping and to go and retain a decent lawyer. From a legal standpoint, I expect the ex-wife's lawyers would be making the most out of her ex-husband's kidnapping attempt to the courts as proof of why he should not have custody of the child.

I have also had clients whose children have been taken to countries in Eastern Europe and have been told by their ex-partners that if they ever entered the respective countries they would be arrested or killed. I told them to consider such threats very seriously as in many places the rights of locals take precedence over the rights of foreigners and law enforcement is for hire or can be paid to ignore things. A thousand dollars or so can influence a judge, put someone in jail, hospital or an unmarked grave.

As for those security and investigation companies claiming to be in the business of recovering children, firstly - apart from advertising they intend to break the law - there are a few other things that can go very, very wrong with their operations. A very well publicized child recovery attempt that went extremely wrong happened in Lebanon in 2016 and was being filmed and documented by a news crew for the Australian "60 Minutes" program. It would have been a very good publicity stunt if it worked but it didn't! The whole crew ended up in jail and could face extradition back to Lebanon on kidnapping charges, not to mention the $2 million it cost the TV company in legal fees!

I have heard stories and seen promotional videos etc. from people claiming to go armed into places like Mexico to rescue children. Well, from a business point of view these clients must have a lot of money to organize the logistics and execute such an operation as they would not be cheap. Also, in most countries, even Mexico, carrying firearms is illegal to start with and where would any weapons come from? Taken illegally from the U.S. or like we see in the movies bought in some shady hotel room above a whore bar? Reality check, if you are caught in Mexico with illegal firearms by the police you will go to jail, if you are caught by Cartel members you will be killed. There are numerous incidents of Americans accidentally crossing into Mexico with firearms, none of which end good for them, a highly-publicized incident was of USMC Sgt. Andrew Tahmooressi who spent 214 joyful days in a Mexican jail before being luckily released!

Now even if the child was snatched back successfully, those executing the operation would have committed the crime of kidnapping to start with, which in most places has a lengthy prison term attached. The child might be safely returned to the parent with custody in their respective country who hired you to perform the operation but, any arrest warrants and extradition requests will be in your name, you would have kidnapped the child in the respective country. When you combine the risk of being arrested, ending up in jail and the child being physically or psychologically harmed during the snatch, things are better left to embassy staff and trusted local attorneys.

As I always say and tell my clients, they need do everything they can to avoid any problematic situations. If a parent is involved in a child custody dispute, especially with a foreign national they need to always consider the worst-case scenarios and put procedures in place, so an abduction cannot happen and if it does law enforcement and the legal authorities are alerted ASAP.

CHILD KIDNAPPING PREVENTION

I wrote this chapter as an article for the "Counter Terrorist" magazine which was published in 2017 and again it is aimed at security professionals and those in the kidnap and ransom industry but is still applicable to parents and care givers. This chapter will provide tips on how to help protect your children from kidnappers and predators.

Child kidnapping prevention

Over the past couple of decades kidnapping and hostage taking have become a booming multimillion-dollar business. Unlike the movies you do not need to be high profile or a high roller to be kidnapped, it can happen to virtually anyone for a multitude of reasons. In the emerging markets of the Middle East, Latin America and Africa business owners within the middle class are often the main targets for criminal gangs. Children are especially vulnerable to kidnapping as their natural inquisitiveness can be exploited, most nannies or drivers are not security trained, and also many kindergartens and schools have very low standards of security.

Most people think of kidnap for ransom situations when we discuss kidnapping, but another type of domestic kidnapping is where an estranged parent will take a child they do not have legal custody for. These situations can become very complicated if the child is taken to or is in another country, as the local laws usually take precedence.

Kidnapping situations are nasty situations to be involved in and best avoided at all costs, period! If the kidnappers are professionals there is a good chance that a hostage would be released when the ransom demands are met, on the other side of the coin if the ransom demands are not met, it would be a good business practice to execute the hostage, to encourage future payments. The professionalism of kidnappers varies greatly from those that are highly skilled to Neanderthals; all, however, are capable of extreme violence.

The express kidnappers for example are generally not what could be classed as high-end criminals. This means they tend to be more violent and unpredictable than groups that target higher profile victims for large ransoms. As always, if ransoms are paid in express kidnappings there is no guarantee the victim will be released, especially if the victims can identify the criminals or have been sexually assaulted, which can be expected in most cases.

We have been approached quite a few times by the families of kidnapping victims wanting to know if we provide hostage rescue services. Of course, our answer is always NO! People that claim to provide such services tend to live in their own little fantasy worlds. There are those claiming to provide such services in places like Mexico; well if you follow the news then you will see that a few times every year Americans are arrested and sent to jail for crossing the Mexican border with a firearm. So, you think the Mexican police, military and the drug cartels will turn a blind eye to a private SWAT team waltzing across the border to save a damsel in distress? I am also sure if they made it back the FBI would be having a chat and ATF would be interested in the weapons crossing the border etc. etc. Also, from a business point of view, consider how much would you charge to go into Mexico to perform a completely illegal operation, face a slow imaginative death, life in a Mexican prison and don't forget the repercussions to you, your family if the Cartels found out you messed with them? As I said, some people tend to live in their own little fantasy worlds, right!

I can't overemphasize why kidnapping situations should be avoided and where a threat is identified precautions need to be taken, especially when children are involved. In most cases children are a lot more vulnerable, easier to take than an adult yet the threat to them is often taken lightly or ignored! Here I am going to list some basic considerations to help prevent child kidnappings.

- **Compile a threat assessment:** This is the most basic and often overlooked element to any security program. You need to consider all the potential threats to the child and get the opinions of others; forget the "it will never happen to me" attitude. Arrogance is the greatest weakness in all security and military operations. Ask opinions from a wide variety of people, advice from security professionals can be helpful but in a lot of instances their opinions are text book and one dimensional. Criminals don't have text books, so also ask those who you think can give you some unique perspectives.
- **How would you kidnap the child?** Think like the kidnappers, think with a criminal's mindset where the rule of law means as little as the life of someone who got in your way! Once you have answered this question and have the threat assessment compiled, then you can start to consider what security measures to put in place to counter the potential threats.

- **Residential security:** It's a sad fact that a lot of kidnappings take place at the victim's residence or when they are entering or exiting. The security of the residence, the grounds and the surrounding area need to be assessed. Contingency plans need to be put in place for potential threat situations and active kidnapping attempts.
- **Pretext tests:** Consider testing the security of the residence and alertness of the staff by sending someone to try and gain entry to the house, grounds or to deliver an unsolicited gift of a toy or sweets for the child. When selecting someone for the pretext remember that people are usually suspicious of young men, not so much of young girls and women with children.
- **Could the child be drugged?** This can be from unsolicited gifts delivered to the house or given while the child is in the garden for an outing. If the child has taken ill the parents' and staff's main concern will be the child's wellbeing and security precautions can be disregarded. The ploy of poisoning the child can be used to get them out of a secure residence for a street kidnapping or to a hospital where a low level of security may exist as a visual deterrent but nothing more.
- **House staff:** Have all house staff been vetted and at least briefed on security awareness and procedures? Criminals will look to recruit or blackmail employees to provide itineraries and sensitive information, that's why you must insure that all your employees are vetted out, supervised and all sensitive information is kept on a need to know basis.
- **Nannies:** The child's nanny will need to be trusted at a far greater level that the other house staff and understand any potential threats the other staff may not have been made aware of. The nanny will need to know how to spot any potential threats and how to respond to any emergency situations.
- **Drivers:** Full time drivers should be trained to identify and react to potential threats and hostile situations. Contract drivers should not be trusted and not be given the details of any trips until the last minute.
- **Security personnel:** Will they fight, run or are they working with the kidnappers. Just because someone has a gun it does not mean it works, they can use it or would use it if they had to. Yes, I am very cynical about those in the security industry and with good reason! Make sure you're not wasting your money!
- **Visitors to the residence:** Ensure visitors are known, contractors have appointments and are not left unattended.
- **School security:** Most schools have minimal security in place, they may have cameras and employ a few guards but nothing that could prevent a kidnapping attempt from a determined semi-professional criminal gang. The issue with armed school security is how they would react to a hostile

incident and are they properly trained? You don't want them shooting a child "by accident" as they try to prevent a kidnapping.

- **School staff:** Are they security aware and trained to deal with emergency situations?
- **Penetration tests:** Consider sending someone to test the school's security; can they get in, walk around unchallenged, talk to children etc.
- **Being picked up from school:** What are the procedures for the children when being picked up from school? What chances are there for the child to be picked up by an unauthorized person? Test it!
- **The child's friends:** What threats could the child's friends be under that could lead to your child being threatened? If your child is visiting friends what are the other family's security precautions like, consider pretexting or a penetration test! We are talking about a child's security, so don't worry about hurting the other parents' feelings, better that than dealing with a kidnapping, right?
- **The child:** When old enough basic security procedures should be taught to the child but be mindful to do it in such a way not to scare them, but to educate them. This needs to be an ongoing process and as they grow they need to be made aware of the potential threats they could encounter both criminal and social!

Hopefully you can see from this chapter there is a lot more to a security program than hiring a big guy with a gun, and we have not touched on such things as local laws, budget, environment and cultural issues etc. Where a potential kidnapping threat is identified everything must be done to minimalize it, if in the process you hurt some people's feelings then so be it. That's a far better state of affairs than to have to pick up the pieces from the aftermath of a kidnapping situation!

AUTHOR

Orlando's experience in risk management business started in 1988 when he enlisted in the British Army and volunteered for a 22-month operational tour in Northern Ireland in an infantry unit. This tour of duty gave him among other things an excellent grounding in anti-terrorist operations. He then joined his unit's Reconnaissance Platoon where he undertook intensive training in small-unit warfare and also undertook training with specialist units such as the RM Mountain and Arctic Warfare Cadre and US Army's Special Forces.

Since leaving the British army in 1993 he has initiated, provided and managed an extensive range of specialist security, investigation and tactical training services to international corporate, private and government clients. Some of these services have been the first of their kind in the respective countries.

His experience has included providing close protection for Middle Eastern Royal families and varied corporate clients, specialist security and asset protection, diplomatic building and embassy security, kidnap and ransom services, corporate investigations and intelligence, para-military training for private individuals and specialist tactical police units and government agencies. Over the years, he has become accustomed to the types of complications that can occur, when dealing with international law enforcement agencies and the problem of organized crime.

Orlando is the chief consultant for Risks Incorporated and is also a published author, writer and photographer and has been interviewed and written articles for numerous media outlets ranging from the New York Times to Soldier of Fortune Magazine on topics ranging from kidnapping, organized crime, surveillance to maritime piracy.

Printed in Great Britain
by Amazon